WRITE A SONNET ON IT!

•

A Hands-On Guide

Wayne Kime

© 2013 by Wayne R. Kime. All rights reserved
ISBN 978-1-304-12401-2

Contents

	Page
Preface	v
Introduction	9
Chapter 1. Words and Phrases	11
Chapter 2. Lines and Rhymes	18
Chapter 3. A Dozen Sonnets	29
Chapter 4. Word Shifts and Shades of Meaning	42
Chapter 5. Another Dozen Sonnets	53
Chapter 6. Groups of Lines	65
Chapter 7. Drafting and Revising	77
Chapter 8. One Last Dozen Sonnets	96
Chapter 9. Coda	109

Preface

In recent years I have thought that a focused, accessible little book like this would be a welcome addition to the literature of creative writing. Friends have agreed, but what at last determined me to write the chapters that follow was a succession of blank looks I noticed among friends and relatives who had expressed pleasure at reading–of all things–my annual Christmas letters. When I remarked that composing them was not that difficult, rather like writing a sonnet, they seemed not to comprehend me.

Evidently writing sonnets is not something we even think about nowadays, I reflected to myself, and yet there are good reasons why we should. We value self-awareness and mindfulness, as deepened by meditation, or journalizing, or exploratory group conversations. We like to express ourselves, broadcasting our thoughts and the details of our lives through social media outlets and self-publishing. We favor short forms of expression–Tweets, short-short fiction, haiku, sound bites, YouTube skits, abbreviations, icons. Then too, many of us enjoy maintaining our mental fitness by devoting time to amusements such as crossword puzzles, cryptograms, doublecrostics, Sudoku, and memory games.

Sonnet writing harmonizes with all these contemporary habits and tastes, and yet its satisfactions and real rewards have been largely overlooked or forgotten. Why should this be? Some persons may associate the very word *sonnet* with dreary schoolroom hours best left behind. Others may avoid sonnets for their identification with Literature (with a capital L). Still others may regard sonnet writing as a practice of the past–enjoyed by some of our genteel forebears, perhaps, but having no place in modern times.

Whatever the reasons for its partial eclipse, the craft of sonnet writing seems ripe for rediscovery, and the purpose of this volume is facilitate that revival of interest. The book's approach is practical, hands-on. Proceeding in step-by-step fashion, it includes free spaces for practice in composing brief passages and is diversified by groups of sonnets for study and possible imitation. It culminates in a chapter wherein the reader fashions his or her own specimens of the two prevalent sonnet forms, the Shakespearean and the Petrarchan. A final gathering of sonnets–about sonnets and sonnet-writing–leads to a "Coda," which offers comments about the now-completed experiment in authorship, with suggestions about possible next steps.

The sonnet occupies a modest place in the broad field of literary activity, and yet leading writers in English have availed themselves of its limited confines to produce some of their best work. The instincts, abilities, and habits one develops in sonnet writing prove useful for authorship in every other literary genre. In that sense, *Write a Sonnet On It!* should foster further involvement in the writing process generally.

Potential users of this book may be classified according to the Goldilocks formula. Experienced authors who write regularly, and who perhaps have published some of their work, may find themselves "too hot" for it–although veteran practitioners of any discipline do like to review the basics every so often. They understand that another person's approach may prove helpful to them by unearthing new possibilities or yielding fresh insights. Such writers may also find this volume suitable as a resource for use by groups of persons under their guidance.

The readers who are "just right" for the book have never taken up verse writing in any serious way, or else have forgotten much of what happened when they did, and would welcome a refresher. The chapters acquaint or reacquaint writers like these with the concepts and skills they need in order to produce sonnets they can take pride in. The commentary is more suggestive than prescriptive and has been designed to appeal to all readers, whether they make use of the book individually or as part of a group.

Returning to the Goldilocks analogy, I submit that no one of average mental capacity is "too cold" to derive benefit from a book like this. If a person can write English, has access to pencil and paper, and can find some free time, then he or she is fully equipped and ready to go. The "coldest" individuals, the same ones who insist they're "not interested in literature" or "can't write" or "would be ashamed of what they produce," are often the very persons who find themselves most engaged with the writing process, once they commit to an experiment of it

For their encouragement, advice, and assistance in the preparation of this work I am happy to thank Alicia Kime, Emily and Evan Kime, Alison Tartt, Eleanore Hofstetter, and Susan Hamilton. Some of the sonnets in Chapters 3, 6, and 8 are reprinted from texts displayed on the website of Sonnets Central, www.sonnets.org, a unique online resource which I recommend to readers of this volume. To the best of my knowledge and understanding, the texts of all the reprinted sonnets, or parts of sonnets, in the book are in the public domain or are presented in a fashion that constitutes fair use.

Wayne Kime

Write a Sonnet On It!

First Thoughts

"Write a sonnet," you ask? Sorry, that's not my line.

I'm really not what you'd call literary.

In fact, unless forced to it, I too rarely

Even read verse, let alone write it. It's fine,

You hone new skills, exercise the mind

In search of words and rhymes. But I can barely

Set down a prose sentence. Think how scary

To someone like me is this sonnet task you'd assign.

Only fourteen lines of rhyming verse, you say,

And "pentameter"? Well then, I'll give it a try.

Let me think now, what shall I choose as my theme?

Maybe the quiet streets at the end of a day?

Washing the car? A child beginning to cry?

The rising sun? You know, I could write a ream.

Introduction

The word *sonnet* derives from early Italian, *sonetto*, meaning little song, and the tradition of sonnet writing in the European languages is now eight centuries old. Sonnet writers in English began publishing their work in the sixteenth century, and have included some of the most honored names in our literary tradition. The sonnet has proved a highly accommodating poetic form. Its fourteen lines of rhymed pentameter verse can be composed in a reasonably short space of time, but it affords space for the economical development of an extended thought, the description of a scene, or the recounting of an action. Sonnet writers have addressed a myriad of topics–love, friendship, politics, religious belief, the weather, food, painting, conversation, firelight, indecision, effort, inspiration, even sonnets and sonnet writing. They have expressed themselves in every imaginable tone--amusement, arch dismissal, admiration, envy, anger, frustration, wonder, confusion.

Given the long tradition of the sonnet, it might be tempting to conclude that everything worthwhile has already been written–that some author or other has recorded a rhymed reflection on virtually every facet of human affairs. Yet that observation would miss a key point, that what someone else may have written on a subject is not what you or I would write. Our approach to it, our way of expressing it, would be uniquely our own. It's perhaps humbling to consider all the good work that has been accomplished before us, but it certainly need not be daunting. The sonnet we sit down to write today will be an emanation of ourselves, so that an open field for expression awaits us all.

This volume sets forth details about the component parts of sonnets in the belief that the craft of sonnet writing merits our study, both as to the product–a completed work–and also the process of creating it. A well fashioned sonnet can be a statement worth preserving. Shortly after my father died, many years ago, I wrote a sonnet about the inevitable fading from memory of his living presence. I recall some of its phrases even now, but I regret that I no longer possess a copy of the whole piece. For me it captured that intense time just as meaningfully as a photograph–more so, really. Of course, what we write need not be sorrowful, or even "deep." A sonnet captures our response to something that has attracted our attention, and if skillfully written it may also connect with others. Whether we choose to share what we write is a matter for us to decide, of course.

Emily Dickinson, one of America's great poets, wrote more than two thousand poems, but only seven appeared in print during her lifetime.

Sonnet writing yields benefits to those who engage in it, no matter the quality and quantity of what they produce. It enhances our alertness to features of the passing scene that could possibly be captured in words. It affords insight into ourselves–what times of day we're at our best, what topics and tones we gravitate toward, how to stimulate our creative powers. It involves us in focused mental exertion as we search out the right words and attempt to shape them into a satisfactory whole.

Because no two sonnets get written in exactly the same way, composing one is a sort of adventure. It requires skill in scouting the territory ahead as we search out a path from line to line. Sometimes it tests our resourcefulness and our patience, but moments do arrive when shafts of sunlight illuminate a way forward. Throughout our process of discovery we gain new respect for the easy mastery displayed by writers of the past.

The chapters that follow offer a mixture of introductory commentary and occasions for practice in techniques that underlie successful sonnet writing. You are encouraged to make use of the blank spaces on the pages to try your hand at all the exercises involved. The book's treatment moves from small building blocks (syllables, single words) to larger ones (groups of lines, sonnet types). Successive chapters should prepare you to write sonnets in much the same way stretching and flexing exercises prepare you for a physical workout. The chapter entitled Drafting and Revising constitutes the full workout–namely, composing two sonnets of your own, one in the Shakespearean pattern, and one in the Petrarchan.

You may never have considered a pursuit like sonnet writing as a particularly good fit for yourself. If so, welcome. When dubious authors begin to experiment with writing, their doubts and reservations tend to melt away. If you do have some past experience in writing and are using this book as a means of taking up where you left off, welcome again. The chapters that follow can do you no harm, and I trust you will find them helpful and not without interest. Finally, if you are already a working writer, welcome again. I have tried to make reading the work an enjoyable experience for all.

Sonnet writing is a small province in the land of literature, but writers who sharpen their skills in it should gain confidence to explore other territory. As you work your way through this treatment of the subject, I hope you will find it stimulating, perhaps on occasion even delightful. To quote a sonnet by William Wordsworth, may you be "Surprised by joy."

Chapter 1. Words and Phrases

The philosopher-poet Samuel Taylor Coleridge once defined poetry in the simplest of terms, as "the best words in the best order." He wrote other, more profound definitions of the term, but this one did focus on the basic tools wielded by sonnet writers–words and word order.

Words

Words pervade our lives, like the air we breathe. Often we don't pay much attention to them, but a moment's thought reveals that they come in all shapes, sizes, flavors, tints, and rhythms. A sonnet writer's first duty is to sustain an alert interest in words.

Studies have shown that in our day-to-day lives we use only a small percentage of the words we know. We may never need to draw upon all those others, but then again we might; and it's helpful to have them within mental reach when we do. As Mark Twain famously observed, the difference between an almost right word and the right one is the difference between a lightning bug and a bolt of lightning. In a small way, I experienced the truth of Twain's observation not long ago, when I was drafting a tribute to a friend. I wanted to characterize in an admiring tone this person's lifelong habit of determined effort, often in the face of continued adversity. Searching my mind, at last I hit upon "unflagging." It wasn't anything unusual, but it was just what I was looking for.

A writer's single best resource for quick reference while at work is a desk dictionary. After all, it's essential that our words mean what we think they do, and the dictionary will clarify any doubts about that. As a tool for finding the *right* words, its usefulness is less obvious. Paging through it for something we think must be there but cannot name, or perhaps spell, is like searching for the proverbial needle in a haystack. Even so, skimming the entries does start the mind on a subliminal quest of its own, and often with a happy result. Whatever we read or hear today may plant seeds for a future unearthing of the exact word we need. The idea is to pay attention to words we encounter, listening to them in our minds, noting the circumstances of their use, and perhaps thereby storing them away in our unconscious. Poets in Old English times, when few persons could read, were said to possess a "word hoard," a verbal storehouse that made possible the verses they recited. In our times, building up a fund of words for possible future use need not be heavy labor. It quickly becomes a pleasant habit, like any other kind of casual collecting.

I admit to a liking for words, especially ones whose sounds seem to me droll in some way. Here are a few, caught in random flight: *aardvark, chatter, bombastic, wily, nozzle, ricochet, snaffle, manicotti.* Now, how about yourself? For starters, think for a few moments and write down some words that appeal to you.

Exactly what was it about the words you chose that caught your fancy? That question can be hard to answer, but try. (If more than one of you are working together, consider sharing your results. The same possibility exists for all the exercises to come.)

Did some of the words you chose strike you as stylish, strange, sexy, raffish, awkward, or what-have-you, but somehow not "sonnetworthy"? Quite possibly so. The question arises, What is appropriate language for use by a sonnet writer? As you may know, dictionary makers classify words in all sorts of ways, notably according to the ordinary circumstances of their use. Ranging from top to bottom, as in a parfait, the traditional levels of usage include formal (on ceremonial occasions), informal (serious but not stuffy discourse), colloquial (as in easy conversation), slang (usually made-up words that quickly go out of fashion), and nonstandard (vulgar terms). It's clear that the partitions dividing these classes of diction are porous, and that not everyone will agree on what label should be associated with a particular word. Dictionaries identify other classes of words, including regional expressions, specialist vocabularies, foreign terms, and neologisms (coinages). Words formerly in use but rarely employed in modern times are known as *archaic*; words passing out of ordinary usage are *obsolescent*; and words found only in literary contexts, such as "Methought," "Forsooth," "Egads," and such, are *literary*.

Absolutely every word in the lexicon, no matter its level of usage, degree of formality, or any other label, is fair game for you as a writer, provided it suits your purpose. Certainly you need not seek out "literary" terms simply because you're writing a sonnet. You may want to lend the piece an antique sound, or a solemn or silly one; and if that's your plan, go for it. In general, the best course now is to write in your own way, given your sense of what you wish to communicate. As in so many other areas of life, such as cooking, dress, driving, and dancing, writers gradually develop their own styles.

One characteristic of words that merits special notice here is their sound. Whatever individual words may mean, when enunciated they create a rhythm and make a kind of music. Non-native speakers have expressed pleasure at hearing the English words *urine, syphilis, enema,* and *cellar door*, and naturally so–they're responding to sounds, not meaning. Among native speakers, sound and meaning go together. As writers we concern ourselves with communicating on both channels, among others to be discussed in later pages. A word that conveys a pleasing combination of sounds is said to be *euphonious*; one whose sounds flow easily is *mellifluous* (from Latin words for the flow of honey). A word whose sounds convey a disharmonious impression is *cacophonous*.

Of course, evaluating the pleasantness or otherwise of a word's sounds is a subjective matter. What may appeal to you may not strike me as favorably. Setting aside for now our individual reactions, some words produce impressions we all agree upon. Words like *nicknack, picnic,* and *chitchat* impose a staccato rhythm. Others like *aphrodisiac* or *parallelism* or *tyrannosaurus* take us on a sort of ride, with loops and slides of sound. Words whose sounds imitate what they refer to are called *onomatopoetic*; think of *sizzle, rat-a-tat, shriek, bumblebee*. Some words almost, but not quite, suggest a sense impression that connects with the things they refer to. For example, consider *blur, roar, luminescent, sear, rumble*. Often it's next to impossible to untangle our responses to the words we hear or read. Nevertheless, we need to be sensitive to the rich sets of responses words evoke. We're in search of the best words in the best order.

Take a few moments to ransack your word stock in search of euphonious, mellifluous, and cacophonous words, words that convey a distinctive rhythm, and onomatopoetic or almost-onomatopoetic words.

A dictionary lists only the *denotations* of words–that is, their intellectual meaning. It does not list their *connotations*–all the associations and implications that contribute to the whole impression they produce. Your dictionary might define *politician* as "an elected or appointed official who is involved with the processes of government." But many other ideas and judgments connect themselves with that word! Or take *bachelor*, which signifies "an unmarried man." To some persons the connotations of *bachelor* might include a carefree life, lots of socializing, and unwillingness to make personal commitments. Others would regard it differently, as suggesting loneliness, lack of direction, and emotional immaturity. The connotations of a word vary not only from person to person, but also as the times change. Consider *stewardess*: once the word connoted glamor, exciting places, and the good life generally, but not any longer. Nowadays one probably thinks of job stress and hard work for indifferent pay. I recently heard a coinage, *airwaitress*, used as a putdown.

Words are not simple building blocks, like bricks; rather, they're slippery and complicated, and they evolve. We need not concern ourselves overmuch about the possibility that the connotations of a word will evolve over time; after all, there's next to nothing we can do about it. Living and writing now, our job is to stay sensitive to the English language as we know it. We guide our readers by selecting words with connotations and sounds that harmonize with our intention, or else, in the case of words whose overtones may prove distracting, by establishing contexts that make our intentions clear.

Consider the connotations of the words below. Have they changed during your lifetime?

| lesbian | suburban | intellectual | do-it-yourself |
| alternative | debtor | homeless | assertiveness |

Two additional ways of classifying words need attention before we move on to phrases. Nouns, words designating "persons, places or things," describe either *abstract* or *concrete* entities and are *general* or *specific* in their range of reference. A general term designates all members of a particular class, such as *automobile, fruit, performance artist*. A more specific term refers to a subclass: *Toyota, melon, ropewalker*. Another step toward particulars takes us to *Toyota Corolla, cassava melon, and Niagara Falls ropewalker*. All the levels of generality have their usefulness, but note that as we approach specific persons, places, and things our minds come into more immediate contact with the physical world–sights, sounds, dimensions. Fine poems are written every day on general themes, but it's good to remember that references to the sensuous world of specifics help bring life and texture to anything we write.

Abstract terms, such as *love, honor, wonder, forgiveness*, and *guilt*, refer to entities that have no physical existence. In contrast, concrete terms refer to things that exist in physical reality. Concrete terms may be general or specific in their scope, but they all designate features of the world we share: canvas, sunset, stone, toenails, the trees seen through the kitchen window. An *image* is a representation of any object that we perceive through our senses.

Just as with the general-specific distinction, both abstract and concrete words have their value. But there is a difference between the two sets of words. Whereas, for example, a definite line of shared identification connects *fruit* to *melon* to *cassava melon*, when we move from the abstract to the concrete we move through uncharted territory. Take *love*, for example. We may think of kinds of love, as that for young children, between young persons, for one's country, or for memory of a place or time. All these take us from the general, *love*, to something more specific; and yet, as words alone, none of more specific concepts connect us with concrete reality. To make that last connection, something like an image needs to be supplied. Abstractions like *love* or *tenderness* or *respect* convey at best a soft-focus meaning when used by themselves. This is good news for the producers of greeting cards, who market their wares to anyone who will purchase them, but it should be a caution to the rest of us. A writer makes abstract ideas real by representing them in concrete terms.

Sonnet-writing requires us to make every word count, to waste no space. Intensives like *awfully, very, really*, and strings of words like *as a matter of fact, on account of,* or *sooner or later* tend to fall by the wayside. This is good verbal discipline.

Phrases

A *phrase* is any group of related words. It might consist of a noun with its adjective attached (*cold comfort*), a preposition with its object (*below ground*), a verb with its adverb (*almost shout*), or any other combination we consider idiomatic–that is, consistent with the way we usually speak and write. Concise phrases tend to prevail in sonnets. War is hell; marriage, purgatory. Youth is certain; age, doubtful. Men marry for [*fill in the blank*]; women, for [*fill in the blank*]. In one variety of sonnet, the Shakespearean, the last two lines actually invite such a formulation. Shakespeare's Sonnet 18, which begins "Shall I compare thee to a summer's day?," ends thus:

> So long as men can breathe, or eyes can see,
> So long lives this, and this gives life to thee.

Repeated phrases–Shakespeare's *So long*, for example–can be useful to show continuity and development within a sonnet. Imagine yourself introducing, say at the beginning or end of every four lines, some phrase like *Not again*, *What comes around*, *Nice try*, *The buzzer sounds*, or *Maybe next time*. The effect would resemble that of a refrain in a song ("The answer, my friend, is blowing in the wind . . ."), drawing attention to the structure you have imposed, and perhaps deepening an impression. You could vary your phrase for an incremental effect: *She looked up*; *She looked down*; *She looked away*.

Try this experiment in the space on the next page: Invent a phrase, then use it at the beginning or end of three or four statements of roughly equal length–say, two sentences each. Vary your repeated phrase a little if you like. Don't worry about writing lines of verse; we'll take that up in the next chapter. To give you an idea of what you are being asked to do, the lines that follow are my own.

> The book sale is tomorrow,
> And I said I'd try to help out. Unfortunately,
> I don't have time.
>
> That movie is playing just three more days,
> And I'd love to see it if I could,
> But there's just no time.
>
> We should eat lunch together more often,
> But something else always comes up.
> It seems we never have time.
>
> It's a wonderful world out there,
> With so much to see and explore,
> If we only had time.

Chapter 2. Lines and Rhymes

The word *verse* derives from a Latin verb meaning "to turn," as in the shift of attention as one line leads to the next in a poem. *Free verse*, increasingly popular in the last century, is "free" of the conventional requirements in other verse forms regarding line length and rhyming. Writers of free verse insist that there's nothing "free" or undisciplined about their lines, whose shape is determined by the organic requirements of each particular statement. On the other hand, the American poet Robert Frost (1874-1963) likened writing it to playing tennis without a net. Excelling in traditional forms and being jealous of his reputation, he looked askance at writers whose practice was different from his own.

Lines

Writers of sonnets and other fixed forms of verse are "free" to write on whatever subject they please, but they work within certain conventions that define those forms. One such convention is line length, as measured by *metrical feet*. The lines of a sonnet are *pentameter* lines, meaning that each consists of five metrical feet. Other popular line lengths are tetrameter, consisting of four feet; trimeter, three feet; and hexameter or Alexandrine, six feet. Several systems for parceling out a line of verse do exist, including counting the stressed syllables or the total number of syllables in it, but we need not concern ourselves with them here.

According to the traditional system for measuring English verse, a metrical foot is a grouping of accented syllables, each marked with a slash ′ above it when analyzed, and unaccented syllables, marked thus ˘. The default rhythm in lines of a sonnet is set by metrical feet called *iambs* (pronounced EYEambs). An iamb consists of one unaccented syllable followed by one accented syllable, ˘ ′, as in *behave* or *insist*. The term *iambic pentameter* refers to lines of verse in which this pattern predominates.

Other types of metrical feet, all of whose names were assigned them by the ancient Greeks, are these:

Trochee (TROWkee), one accented followed by one unaccented syllable, ′ ˘, as in *cabin* or *retro*;

Dactyl (DACKtill), one accented followed by two unaccented syllables, ′ ˘ ˘, as in *watercress* or *out of it*;

Anapest (ANNapest), two unaccented followed by one accented syllable, ˘ ˘ ′, as in *unaware* or *in a flash*;

Spondee (SPAWNdee), two accented syllables, ′ ′, as in *right now* or *big deal*;

Pyrrhic (PIRRik), two unaccented syllables, ˘ ˘, as in *as in* or *of the*.

Spondees do not often appear consecutively, nor do pyrrhic feet. Each of the other four types, especially the iamb, may fill an entire line. For practice, you may want to scan the examples below. Here is an iambic line:

Is this the face that launched a thousand ships?

A trochaic line:

By the shining Big-Sea Water

A dactylic line:

How could you do this to someone you say that you idolize?

An anapestic line:

By the light of the silvery moon.

Most pentameter lines include more than one type of metrical foot. After all, the regular beat of the metronome–tick tock tick tock tick tock–has its use, but its rhythm is not that of speech. Often lines include a marked interruption of their rhythm, known as a *caesura* and shown when analyzed by a double vertical slash ‖ . A single slash | marks the division between one metrical foot and another.

The process of dividing a line into its metrical feet by indicating the accented and unaccented syllables that comprise it is called *scanning*, or *scansion*. The result is a visual representation of the line's *meter*, or internal rhythm. Here are two scanned lines, from "Hymn to Intellectual Beauty," by Percy Bysshe Shelley (1792-1822):

′ ′ | ˘ ′ | ˘ ′ | ˘ ′ | ˘ ′
Love, Hope, and Self- esteem, like clouds depart

′ ˘ ‖ ˘ ′ | ˘ ′ | ˘ ′ | ˘ ′
And come, for some uncertain moments lent.

As this example demonstrates, scanning is not an exact science. In the first line above, one might argue that each of the three commas marks a caesural pause; certainly they slow the pace. Once past "Self-esteem," the pace quickens and the rhythm becomes slightly irregular. In both lines, some syllables are stressed more heavily than others. Scansion fails to take these subtleties into account.

Like the terms we use to designate types of metrical feet, our method of scansion derives from the ancient Greeks, who classified syllables as long or short according to the length of time it took to enunciate them, rather than as accented and unaccented as we do. The ancient system is thus an imprecise tool for use with the English language, although it does accurately reveal the pattern of accented and unaccented syllables within a line.

Because the pentameter line is a basic component of sonnets, you need to develop a facility for "thinking in pentameters." Writing verse well is more complicated than simply arranging patterns of accented and unaccented syllables along a line, but that constructive skill is essential. So, give yourself some practice now in writing lines five metrical feet in length. Write individual lines; don't worry about linking one to the next. You should have no difficulty including the various types of metrical feet, but scan your lines to be sure you've accomplished what you intended.

Scanning lines of verse is a means to an end, not an end in itself. A skillful poet adjusts the sound and rhythm of his or her words to complement the ideas and impressions they convey. Alexander Pope (1688-1744), a master of this exacting craft, expressed the idea in his "An Essay on Criticism":

> True ease in writing comes from art, not chance,
> As those move easiest who have learned to dance.
> 'Tis not enough no harshness give offense,
> The sound must seem an echo to the sense.

Pope also understood that deviations from a pattern of dance steps, or any other norm, will stand out, for better or worse. Imitating poets who neglect to shape their lines with due care, he wrote a sequence of pentameter lines that, for no good reason, lapse into hexameter, or Alexandrine:

> A needless Alexandrine ends the song,
> That, like a wounded snake, drags its slow length along.

If you scan that last line, you'll find that its six-foot length combines with the image of the snake, the accented word *drags*, and the spondaic *slow length* to convey the impression Pope intends, of something needlessly and drearily drawn out.

Of course, variation from the pentameter pattern need not always be a flaw. Because it draws attention to itself, it may be useful for emphasis. A line that lacks all or part of a metrical foot, or that adds one, provides its author an opportunity not available through adherence to the prevailing line length.

An analysis of Shakespeare's Sonnet 129 will show how he causes the sound and rhythm of his lines to interact with the meaning of his words to convey the essence of his subject–in this case, lust. Read the sonnet aloud, or recite it in your mind. Nothing is mellifluous here; the sounds are harsh, the rhythm nervous, insistent; the balanced statements are definitive, absolute. Sound and sense, form and content, are one. Scan the lines to see how their rhythm contributes to the poem's effect.

Th' expense of spirit in a waste of shame

Is lust in action; and till action, lust

Is perjured, murderous, bloody, full of blame,

Savage, extreme, rude, cruel, not to trust;

Enjoyed no sooner but despiséd straight:

Past reason hunted; and no sooner had,

Past reason hated, as a swallowed bait,

On purpose laid to make the taker mad:

Mad in pursuit, and in possession so;

Had, having, and in quest to have, extreme;

A bliss in proof, and proved, a very woe;

Before, a joy proposed; behind, a dream;

All this the world well knows; yet none knows well

To shun the heaven that leads men to this hell.

Rhymes

Another basic feature of sonnets is their rhyme scheme–the pattern of repeated sounds at the ends of lines. In recent times some poets have actually dispensed with rhyme in their sonnets, sacrificing that musical effect and some of the graceful verbal footwork that makes it possible. But they are rare exceptions. The traditional idea of a sonnet as including an arrangement of rhymes has taken deep root.

The effort to find rhymes that carry forward one's thought can be a teasing challenge. No single approach to the task works for everyone, nor always for anyone. As with one's search for exactly the right word, various printed resources can be helpful. A rhyming dictionary, for example, may not guarantee a good result, but looking through it helps us search territory we don't traverse in conscious thought. It's as if we shine a flashlight at random into a dark place whose shape and dimensions we don't know. What we find there will be a discovery–quite possibly not quite what we are looking for, but stimulating nevertheless and potentially useful later on. Some writers jot down lists of rhyme words before they begin composing–*carrier*, *terrier*, *ferryer*, *barrier*, *merrier*, *Perrier*, *harrier*, for example–to help get started. "Whatever works" is the best motto here.

In an essay entitled "The Figure a Poem Makes," Robert Frost described the experience of searching one's way into and through a poem. "It is but a trick poem and no poem at all if the best of it was thought of first and saved for the last," he wrote. Instead, composition "must be a revelation, or a series of revelations, as much for the poet as for the reader." The poem gradually assumes its shape, and as it does so one discovers what he or she has to say.

Sonnets often include rhyme sounds in the midst of lines that anticipate sounds at their ends or echo preceding lines, a feature known as *internal rhyme*. *End rhyme* is the standard, of course, and the pattern of a sonnet's end rhymes is what determines its classification as of one traditional type or another. Rhymes that fall on the stressed, final syllable of words are called *masculine rhymes;* some examples are *erect, confect, infect, detect*. Two-syllable rhymes that fall on unaccented final syllables are known as *feminine*, as in *lettuce* and *met us, darken* and *harken*. (The designations as *masculine* and *feminine* invite an explanation. If you speak out the masculine rhymes above, you'll find they have a forceful, assertive feel to them. The feminine rhymes exhibit a certain lightness. Such as it is, that's the explanation.)

Half-rhyme, also known as *off-rhyme*, occurs when pairs of words include rhyming sounds that are not quite identical, as *terry* and *tarry*, or *ginger* and *pincer*. *Eye-rhyme* signifies words that are spelled as if their rhymes were exact but that sound differently when pronounced, as *catch* and *watch*, or *shove* and *move*. *Consonance* is end-rhyme in which the stressed final consonants agree but the vowels that precede them do not, as *turn* and *tarn*, or *thimble* and *bumble*. All these forms of imperfect rhyme produce a marked variation from the regular rhyme pattern, a form of *dissonance* or disharmony. From a reader's point of view, it can be satisfying to observe how the end rhymes in a poem seem to present themselves so neatly and ingeniously, as if without effort. At the same time, something that rings as a variation from pure rhyme can yield its own pleasing effect.

Two other types of repeated sound should be mentioned here, even though they occur both within rhymes and outside them. One is *alliteration*, the repetition of consonant sounds, as in *really rough rider* or *tattered tonsils*. The other is *assonance*, the repetition of vowel sounds, as in *apt slap* or *teensy weensy*.

"Do we have to know all these terms about rhymes?" you may ask at this point. "Will they be on the test?" Well, first as to the "test": In this book there's no test, here or hereafter. The practical exercises you encounter are developmental exercises, or creative amusements if you prefer, or perhaps enthusiasms in embryo, but not "tests." Second, as to knowing "all these terms": What's important as takeaway from the preceding paragraphs is your developing a sensitivity to the effects the different sorts of rhymes can produce, and when to use them. Whether you memorize their names is a different matter. Still, if you wish to share with others your ideas about your work as a writer, it's useful to have access to a common vocabulary. Specialist terminology is a mark of every discipline.

On the next page is a creative problem for your amusement and practical instruction.

First look over the four lines of rhyme words below, left to right:

bottle	dazzle	fizzle	fossil	wassail	dimple	passel
skunk	monk	funk	wonk	spelunk	Podunk	slack
chance	lapdance	alliance	once	romance	demands	sands
spaghetti	machete	petty	already	confetti	Serengeti	pity

Now, selecting one of the lists, in the space below write four lines of verse, approximately equal in length, using a different one of the listed words as an end rhyme in each, and causing your statement to make approximate sense. For extra credit, write pentameter lines. To win a gold star, upgrade to five lines.

This practice session is open-ended, so the pages that follow are blank. Once you've finished a response using one of the four sets of rhyme words, try producing something different using other words in that set. Or, try scrambling the sequence of rhyme words in the first lines you wrote. This exercise helps build verbal dexterity and promotes a habit of stretching for ideas. Go on to another list of rhyme words if you want, and perhaps write two responses to it, one grave and one gay. Or, mix and match words from different lists; insert a new rhyme word as necessary; repeat a rhyme if you want, perhaps using it in a different sense. Move things around, experiment.

-------- 27 --------

Chapter 3. A Dozen Sonnets

Here is a sampler of sonnets–some well known, some not–written from the sixteenth through the twentieth century. The poems suggest the thematic range sonnet writers have explored during that period, and they may also give you some ideas about subjects for your writing and techniques for developing them. After all, imitation is a form of compliment. Try not to read the sonnets simply for "what they're about." It's natural to focus on the subject matter of any writing we take up, but these poems will reward your closer study. Scan some lines if you're so inclined, and note any mannerisms of style that stand out. For your convenience in observing details and tracing relationships, the sonnets are printed with extra spacing in and around them. We will refer to some of them in the chapter that follows.

Edmund Spenser (1552-1599)

Happy, ye leaves, when as those lily hands
Which hold my life in their dead-doing might
Shall handle you, and hold in love's soft bands,
Like captives trembling at the victor's sight;
And happy lines! on which, with starry light,   5
Those lamping eyes will deign sometimes to look,
And read the sorrows of my dying spright
Written with tears in heart's close-bleeding book;
And happy rhymes! Bathed in the sacred brook
Of Helicon, whence she derivéd is;–   10
When ye behold that angel's blessed look,
My soul's long-lackéd food, my heaven's bliss,
Leaves, lines, and rhymes, seek her to please alone,
Whom if we please, I care for other none.

Line 7, spright: spirit.
Line 10, Helicon: A mountain in central Greece, Helicon was the legendary home of the Muses and sacred to Apollo, the god of wisdom, poetry, and prophesy.

Sir Walter Ralegh (1552-1618)

Three things there be that prosper up apace
And flourish, whilst they grow asunder far,
But on a day, they meet all in one place,
And when they meet, they one another mar;
And they be these: the wood, the weed, the wag.   5
The wood is that which makes the gallow tree,
The weed is that which strings the hangman's bag,
The wag, my pretty knave, betokeneth thee.
Mark well, dear boy, whilst these assemble not,
Green springs the tree, hemp grows, the wag is wild;   10
But when they meet, it makes the timber rot,
It frets the halter, and it chokes the child.
Then bless thee, and beware, and let us pray
We part not with thee at this meeting day.

Sir Philip Sidney (1554-1586)

Leave me, O Love, which reachest but to dust,
And thou, my mind, aspire to higher things;
Grow rich on that which never taketh rust;
Whatever fades, but fading pleasure brings.
Draw in thy beams, and humble all thy might   5
To that sweet yoke where lasting freedoms be,
Which breaks the clouds and opens forth the light,
That doth both shine and give us light to see.
O take fast hold; let that light be thy guide
In this small course which birth draws out to death,   10
And think how evil becometh him to slide
Who seeketh heaven, and comes of heavenly breath.
Then farewell, world; thy uttermost I see:
Eternal Love, maintain thy life in me.

Henry Moore (1732-1802)

Gold

Almighty gold! whose magic charms dispense
Worth to the worthless, to the graceless grace,
To cowards valour, and to blockheads sense,
And to the withered maid a Hebe's face.
Poor love exiled, thou sitst on Hymen's throne;   5
Thou rulest the court, the senate, and the bar;
And though the church thy deity disown,
Some whisper thou hast priest and altar there.
All human charities, all laws divine
Deluded mortals offer at thy shrine;   10
O thou supreme, like fate, to kill or save!
To thy vast empire what is wanting more?
"Nought," sighs Avaro, "had it but the power
To silence conscience, and to bribe the grave."

Line 4, Hebe: In Greek mythology, Hebe is the goddess of youth, cupbearer to the gods.
Line 5, Hymen: The god of marriage.
Line 13, Avaro: An invented name, from Latin *avarus*, greedy, as in *avarice*.

Samuel Taylor Coleridge (1772-1834)

Work Without Hope
Lines composed 21ˢᵗ February 1825

All Nature seems at work. Slugs leave their lair–
The bees are stirring–birds are on the wing–
And Winter slumbering in the open air
Wears on his smiling face a dream of Spring!
And I the while, the sole unbusy thing,   5
Nor honey make, nor pair, nor build, nor sing.

Yet well I ken the banks where amaranths blow,
Have traced the fount where streams of nectar flow.
Bloom, O ye amaranths! bloom for whom ye may,
For me ye bloom not! Glide, rich streams, away!   10
With lips unbrightened, wreathless brow, I stroll:
And would you learn the spells that drowse my soul?
Work without Hope draws nectar in a sieve,
And Hope without an object cannot live.

Line 7, amaranths: Plants that do not fade, and so symbolize immortality and everlasting beauty.
Line 8, nectar: In Greek mythology, nectar is the favored drink of the gods.
Line 11, wreathless brow: A brow not decorated with a laurel wreath, in ancient times a symbol of honor awarded to poets and heroes.

William Cullen Bryant (1794-1878)

To Cole, The Painter, Departing for Europe

Thine eyes shall see the light of distant skies:
Yet, Cole! thy heart shall bear to Europe's strand
A living image of thy native land,
Such as on thy own glorious canvas lies.
Lone lakes–savannahs where the bison roves–　　　5
Rocks rich with summer garlands–solemn streams–
Skies, where the desert eagle wheels and screams–
Spring bloom and autumn blaze of boundless groves.
Fair scenes shall greet thee where thou goest–fair,
But different–every where the trace of men,　　　10
Paths, homes, groves, ruins, from the lowest glen
To where life shrinks from the fierce Alpine air.
Gaze on them, till the tears shall dim thy sight,
But keep that earlier, wilder image bright.

Title, Cole, The Painter: Thomas Cole (1801-1848), an American landscape painter, founded the Hudson River School, an art movement devoted to representing the grand, unspoiled wilderness of the New World.

Henry Timrod (1829-1867)

Some truths there be are better left unsaid;
Much is there that we may not speak unblamed.
On words, as wings, how many joys have fled!
The jealous fairies love not to be named.
There is an old-world tale of one whose bed
A genius graced, to all, save him, unknown;
One day the secret passed his lips, and sped
As secrets speed–thenceforth he slept alone.
Too much, oh! far too much is told in books;
Too broad a daylight wraps us all and each.
Ah! it is well that, deeper than our looks,
Some secrets lie beyond conjecture's reach.
Ah! it is well that in the soul are nooks
That will not open to the keys of speech.

Christina Rossetti (1830-1894)

In an Artist's Studio

One face looks out from all his canvases,
One selfsame figure sits or walks or leans:
We found her hidden just behind those screens,
That mirror gave back all her loveliness.
A queen in opal or in ruby dress, 5
A nameless girl in freshest summer-greens,
A saint, an angel–every canvas means
The same one meaning, neither more nor less.
He feeds upon her face by day and night,
And she with true kind eyes looks back on him, 10
Fair as the moon and joyful as the light:
Not wan with waiting, not with sorrow dim;
Not as she is, but was when hope shone bright;
Not as she is, but as she fills his dream.

Gerard Manley Hopkins (1844-1889)

God's Grandeur

The world is charged with the grandeur of God.
    It will flame out, like shining from shook foil;
    It gathers to a greatness, like the ooze of oil
Crushed. Why do men then now not reck his rod?
Generations have trod, have trod, have trod;   5
    And all is seared with trade; bleared, smeared with toil;
    And wears man's smudge, and shares man's smell: the soil
Is bare now, nor can foot feel, being shod.

And for all this, nature is never spent;
    There lives the dearest freshness deep down things;   10
And though the last lights off the black West went
    Oh, morning, at the brown brink eastward, springs–
Because the Holy Ghost over the bent
    World broods with warm breast and with ah! bright wings.

Elinor Wylie (1885-1928)

Pretty Words

Poets make pets of pretty, docile words:
I love smooth words, like gold-enameled fish
Which circle slowly with a silken swish,
And tender ones, like downy-feathered birds:
Words shy and dappled, deep-eyed deer in herds,　　　5
Come to my hand, and playful if I wish,
Or purring softly at a silver dish,
Blue Persian kittens, fed on cream and curds.

I love bright words, words up and singing early;
Words that are luminous in the dark, and sing;　　　10
Warm lazy words, white cattle under trees;
I love words opalescent, cool, and pearly,
Like midsummer moths, and honied words like bees,
Gilded and sticky, with a little sting.

Hugh J. Evans*

The Veld

From sky to sky the veld, vast, tawny, bare,
Surrounds me like a vision in a dream,
Mysterious and unreal: no flower or stream,
No friendly smoke or stack is anywhere;
E'en God's own living creatures are not there,–   5
No bird, no bough whereon to perch, no theme
Whereon to sing; to me there only seem
The sun, sky, veld, the light immaculate air.–
Whose great majestic archicraft did raise
This blue-domed temple without priest or psalm,   10
Without a tone of all the diapase,
With unascending incense without balm,
Without a worshipper in prayer or praise,
Mute with an incommunicable calm?

* Biographical data about Hugh J. Evans has not been located. According to the "Sonnets Central" website, www.sonnets.org, from which it is reprinted here, this poem was published in *Sonnets of South Africa*, edited by E. H. Crouch (1911).

Edgell Rickword (1898-1982)

War and Peace

In sodden trenches I have heard men speak,
Though numb and wretched, wise and witty things;
And loved them for the stubbornness that clings
Longest to laughter when Death's pulleys creak;

And seeing cool nurses move on tireless feet   5
To do abominable things with grace,
Deemed them sweet sisters in that haunted place
Where, with child's voices, strong men howl or bleat.

Yet now these men lay stubborn courage by,
Riding dull-eyed and silent in the train   10
To old men's stools; or sell gay-coloured socks
And listen fearfully for Death; so I
Love the low-laughing girls, who now again
Go daintily, in thin and flowing frocks.

Chapter 4. Word Shifts and Shades of Meaning

Sonnets reward focused attention in ways that casual reading and conversation do not. We now take up some additional features of their complex mode of communication, variations from normal word order and the use of words in ways that differ from normal practice.

Word Shifts

In this section we draw upon the sonnets in the previous chapter for examples of the techniques being described.

Sonnets often announce their structure and emphasize their themes through *repetition*. Thus the sonnet by Edmund Spenser (page 30) uses *happy* in its lines 1, 5, 9, at the beginning of each four-line grouping. Then, *Leaves, lines, and rhymes*, which appear individually in those lines, are repeated together in line 13. Sir Walter Ralegh's poem (page 31) wittily employs a similar technique with the word *wag* and other repeated *w* sounds. Christina Rossetti (page 37) builds her effect by repeating *one* in the initial lines, then rounds it out in the last three, each of which begins *Not*. William Cullen Bryant (page 35) makes effective use of the dashes that separate phrases in lines 5-7 of his poem; he causes them to suggest expansiveness, as on a painter's canvas.

Parallelism, a repetition of grammatical structure, can deepen an impression. The repeated *to* phrases in lines 2 through 4 of Henry Moore's sonnet (page 33) draw ironic attention to the transmuting power of gold. The concluding interjections in Henry Timrod's piece (page 36) return us to his first line and emphasize its importance. In Gerard Manley Hopkins' sonnet (page 38), lines 2 and 3 instance God's irrepressible grandeur by clauses that begin *It* and conclude with images that begin *like*.

The *catalog*, a listing of elements that are presented as related in some way, suggests something overwhelming or inescapable. Line 6 in Moore's sonnet affirms the pervasiveness of gold's dominion over human affairs. Lines 1-4 in Samuel Taylor Coleridge's "Work Without

Hope" (page 34) set forth examples of the author's initial generalization, leading to the portrayal of himself as at odds with all nature. Line 11 of Bryant's poem traces in its monotonous rhythm the pervasiveness of human presence in Europe. Elinor Wylie's entire poem (page 39) catalogs kinds of words, likening them to pets. In a similar way Hugh J. Evans (page 40) evokes the emptiness of the South African veldt by cataloging the signs of life that are absent from it.

Repetition, parallelism, and catalogs lend themselves to sonnet writing because of the economy and consistency of effect they make possible. The same may be said of word arrangements that highlight the relationship between the elements they yoke together. Among these, three should be mentioned: *balance and antithesis*; *inversion*; and *oxymoron*.

In a balanced construction, phrases or clauses are set against each other to indicate a similarity in their meaning. Antithesis occurs when the balanced elements involve a contrast. Lines 7 and 8 of Sir Philip Sidney's "Leave me, O Love" (page 32) are balanced, describing together the good effects of devotion to "higher things." The final line of Moore's "Gold," "To silence conscience and to bribe the grave," is balanced, both parts naming feats that mere gold cannot accomplish. Edgell Rickword's "War and Peace" (page 41) employs antithesis in line 2, describing the unexpected composure of men in a time of intense stress. His whole poem is built on the contrast between men and women during wartime and as they are now.

Inversion, the reversal of usual order in words or phrases, is another device for emphasis. The final line of Spenser's "Happy, ye leaves" shows its effect neatly. From its outset the poem presents exaggeration after exaggeration, but the inverted *other none* at the very end drives home its climactic claim, that the speaker cares for absolutely nothing else than giving pleasure to his lady. In "Pretty Words," Wylie names types of words in the usual adjective-noun order (*smooth words*, line 2; *tender ones*, line 4), then reverses it (*words opalescent*, line 12) or else employs a different construction (*Words that are luminous*, line 10). The effect is of her glancing in this direction, then in another as she pleases herself by characterizing her varied word-pets.

Oxymoron, a form of antithesis much in use by sonnet writers, is a bringing together of seeming opposites to form a paradoxical but valid expression. Examples are "wise fool," "child man," "sad satisfaction." When Moore writes phrases like *To cowards valour, and to blockheads sense* (line 3) he is pointing out the magical potency of gold. When Rickword describes *that haunted place / Where, with child's voices, strong men howl or bleat* (lines 7-8) he conjoins seeming opposites in what might be called a near-oxymoron. (The lines are more effective as they stand than if he had written a pure oxymoron, "strong child men" or something of that kind. They set before us the utter reduction from manhood that prevails among the sufferers.)

Three variations of normal word order–*ellipsis*, *elision*, and *expletives*–help a sonnet writer tailor statements to the pentameter line, and may serve other purposes as well. Ellipsis is the omission of words necessary for grammatical completeness but not for comprehension. Henry Timrod makes use of it with *On words, as wings, how many joys have fled!* (line 2). By omitting "on" from the second phrase he causes the line to flit along rather than to roll itself out, lending its rhythm to the meaning of his words. Elision is the omission of an unstressed syllable, often producing an impression of informal or hurried speech. Examples are *ne'er* for *never*, *th'* for *the*, as in *in th' evening*.

Expletive, in the sense used here, does not refer to slang or other words of doubtful acceptability. It refers instead to words that are not necessary to convey meaning but that lengthen an expression, often to create a slight delay. Ralegh employs in his first line an expletive phrase, *there be that*, that helps establish his tone, as of an old man's good advice. Timrod achieves a similar effect with *there be* in line 1 of his sonnet, adding a note of satisfaction in the wordy phrases–*Ah! it is well that*–in lines 11 and 13. Hopkins begins line 10 of "God's Grandeur" with *There lives*, delaying for a moment his introduction of *the dearest freshness deep down things*, a concept that dominates the rest of his poem. His *Oh* in line 12 and *ah!* in line 14 are not waste words, but expressions of wonder and elation.

Shades of Meaning

Words and phrases used in ways that range outside their literal denotation are known as *figures of speech*. The sonnets in the chapter that follows will reward your close attention to the several figures of speech they incorporate. Read through them now if you like, and then again later. In the remainder of this chapter you will supply your own examples, rather than continuing to draw upon the sonnets in Chapter 3.

Hyperbole, or overstatement, is deliberate exaggeration, something not intended to be taken literally. Here is a comic example: "Ummm! That hot dog deserved five stars from Michelin." Here is something more serious: "When I received the job offer, I felt I could leap to the moon." Your examples:

Understatement, the opposite of hyperbole, is representation of something as less important, weighty, or noteworthy than it is. Like hyperbole, understatement draws attention to the difference between what is stated and the actual fact. Both terms are forms of *irony*. When Ralegh (to glean one more example from Chapter 3) writes that the hangman's noose "chokes the child" (line 12) he understates the matter with grim irony. Your examples of understatement:

An *allusion* is a reference to a person, place, event, or something else that relates in some way relevant to the matter under discussion. If I complain that I feel like Sisyphus when confronting work to clean up my messy yard in springtime, I compare myself to a mythic figure who was doomed to perform the same exhausting task over and over again. Allusions may be explicit, as in the Sisyphus example, or indirect. If you were to write "I'm free at last," you would be alluding indirectly, probably either to a beloved African American spiritual or to a melancholy love song by Hank Williams. Indirect allusions can be doubtful in what they refer to, so it's well to ensure that your rationale for making them is clear.

Write down a few possibilities for allusion in a sonnet you might compose. What would be your subject, and what their relation to it? If you expressed the allusions indirectly, would a reader understand you?

The caution about vague allusions opens up a more positive possibility–namely, the creative use of *ambiguity*. When we rely chiefly on the denotations of words, we place a premium on clarity, definiteness of meaning. But one way in which poetry unfolds its rich pattern of overtones and associations is by the use of words that admit of more than one meaning, leaving any exact significance uncertain. The phrase "free at last," with all it overtones, can suggest escape from enslavement, emptiness at ending a relationship, exhaustion, exhilaration, or something else. Ambiguity can easily pass into obscurity, but when used with tact it heightens the reader's sensitivity to a poem's implications and possible meanings. A prime example of its effective use is a refrain in "The Waking," a poem by Theodore Roethke (1908-1963) about his approach to life: "I wake to sleep, and take my waking slow."

Write a few statements that, if supported by appropriate contexts, could be made creatively ambiguous. If you find yourself at a loss for ideas, look through the sonnets in the next chapter.

The figure of speech most often associated with poetry is *metaphor*, a statement of identity between two entities that are not literally comparable. The creation of a metaphor is an act of imagination–one that Aristotle considered the preeminent faculty of a poet. Metaphor imbues each of its referents with the qualities and emotional aura of the other, drawing attention to their actual, though not literal, similarities. My body is not literally a house, but when I lament that "this old house" is getting old and creaky, I am readily understood. Similarly, if we read of a plant stretching its fingers deep into the ground, we understand what is meant–an identification between the plant and a human being. The same perception underlies phrases such as "the sea moaned" or "the family cabin slept through the winter." Like allusions, metaphors may be explicit or else indirect, implied. If I observe that my friend Fred "wagged his tail and whined," I imply that he is a dog–not just doglike, but a dog. If I wish to be direct, I refer to him as "my puppy, Fred." Obviously a metaphor can have a powerful impact.

Before we take up some special varieties of metaphor, write out a few of your own, direct and implied. First decide on a person, place, or thing that will serve as the basis of your imaginative connection, then find words or phrases to suit the identification you intend. Try to steer clear of clichés like "This old house."

Types of metaphor often encountered in sonnets are *personification*, direct or implied; *metonymy*; *synecdoche*; *allegory*; and *symbol*. Personification, as the word implies, is the attribution of humanity to something nonhuman. When I begin a poem "Debt! why must you shadow my every step?," I address Debt as if it were a person. This sort of direct address, by the way, is known as *apostrophe*. Personification is a simple but powerful means of drawing attention to one's theme.

Metonymy and synecdoche go together in the minds of most persons. Metonymy is the substitution of words associated with a thing for direct reference to the thing itself. When we write "Rome has announced a revision of its teaching" on an item of belief, we don't mean that the city itself did so; we mean that the Holy See, located in the Vatican State enclosed by Rome, did so, and our meaning is clear. Synecdoche involves reference to a part to signify the whole, or else the reverse, reference to the whole to signify a part. If you tell me, "That's a nice set of wheels you have," you are complimenting me on my automobile, not on its four wheels; you substitute a part for the whole. If you warn me, "Watch out–here comes the law!" you probably refer to police car, or a police officer; you substitute the whole for a part.

Allegory is the elaboration of a metaphor that involves a point-by-point set of symbolic relationships. In a famous sonnet, John Donne likens himself to a piece of iron that needs to be battered into shape by God the blacksmith, smashed and broken to be made new. Another seventeenth century writer, George Herbert, portrays himself as a tenant who seeks a new lease from a rich landholder, whose manor is in heaven, and is granted it at the moment of the landholder's violent death. Allegory is no longer in fashion, and can be difficult to elaborate within the confines of a sonnet, but it is inherently dramatic and can create a powerful effect.

A symbol is a physical object that is portrayed literally but that suggests additional associations. Its significance within a poem is open-ended, being controlled by its context. Thus a rose might have romantic, funereal, religious, or simply decorative significance, depending on how it is presented. A door closed or left slightly ajar might be symbolic, as might a darkened room, or an unopened envelope. Symbols need to be introduced with caution, but they can enrich a poet's treatment. No one who has read Coleridge's poem forgets the image of the albatross hung round the neck of the ancient mariner.

The final figure of speech for introduction here is *simile*, an affirmed connection between unlike things on the basis usually of a single feature or quality they share. Most often similes are introduced by the words *like*, *as*, or *as if*. As with metaphor, a simile links one's responses to the two objects it connects. A sonnet by D. H. Lawrence (1885-1930), "Baby Running Barefoot," consists almost entirely of similes:

> When the white feet of the baby beat across the grass
> The little white feet nod like white flowers in a wind,
> They poise and run like puffs of wind that pass
> Over water where the weeds are thinned.
>
> And the sight of their white playing in the grass
> Is winsome as a robin's song, so fluttering;
> Or like two butterflies that settle on a glass
> Cup for a moment, soft little wing-beats uttering.

> And I wish that the baby would tack across here to me
>
> Like a wind-shadow running on a pond, so she could stand
>
> With two little bare white feet upon my knee
>
> And I could feel her feet in either hand
>
> Cool as syringa buds in morning hours,
>
> Or firm and silken as young peony flowers.

The watery scene, the insubstantial wind, the bird's song, the fluttery movements of the butterflies, and the textures of the flowers become as it were parts of the little girl's spirit and physical presence.

"Baby Running Barefoot" demonstrates a point for special emphasis. The variations from ordinary language we have been noticing in this chapter are <u>not</u> merely decorations, but are integral parts of the poems that incorporate them. Without them, the poems would lose some of their life.

As a final example, here is the initial stanza of "First Love," a three-stanza poem by John Clare (1793-1864):

> I ne'er was struck before that hour
>   With love so sudden and so sweet,
> Her face it bloomed like a sweet flower
>   And stole my heart away complete.
> My face turned pale as deadly pale.   5
>   My legs refused to walk away,
> And when she looked, what could I ail?
>   My life and all seemed turned to clay.

These ostensibly simple lines incorporate many of the devices we have noticed, including the simile in line 3, the personification in line 6, and the de-personification (as it were) in line 8. Note, too, the expletive "it" in line 3, how it changes the rhythm and highlights the words before and after it. The entire stanza is hyperbolic–and yet why not, given its subject? Fond, wondrous, and just a bit comical, the lines seem quite natural but are clearly artful. Without the figurative expressions he selected, Clare's evocation of "love so sudden and so sweet" would be a poorer product.

A sonnet by John Clare is among those in the next chapter.

Use this page and the one that follows to experiment with any or all of personification, metonymy, synecdoche, allegory, symbol, and simile.

Chapter 5. Another Dozen Sonnets

John Donne (1572-1631)

Batter my heart, three-personed God; for You
As yet but knock, breathe, shine, and seek to mend;
That I may rise and stand, o'erthrow me, and bend
Your force to break, blow, burn, and make me new.
I, like an usurped town, to another due, 5
Labor to admit You, but O, to no end;
Reason, Your viceroy in me, me should defend,
But is captíved, and proves weak or untrue.
Yet dearly I love you, and would be lovéd fain,
But am betrothed unto Your enemy. 10
Divorce me, untie or break that knot again;
Take me to You, imprison me, for I
Except you enthrall me, never shall be free,
Nor ever chaste, except You ravish me.

John Milton (1608-1674)

How soon hath Time, the subtle thief of youth,
    Stoln on his wing my three and twentieth year!
    My hasting days fly on with full career,
    But my late spring no bud or blossom shew'th.
Perhaps my semblance might deceive the truth,   5
    That I to manhood am arrived so near,
    And inward ripeness doth much less appear,
    That some more timely-happy spirits endu'th.
Yet be it less or more, or soon or slow,
    It shall be still in strictest measure even   10
    To that same lot, however mean or high,
Toward that which Time leads me, and the will of Heaven;
    All is, if I have grace to use it so,
    As ever in my great Taskmaster's eye.

Line 5, semblance might deceive: appearance might not show

William Wordsworth (1770-1850)

Composed upon Westminster Bridge, September 3, 1802

Earth has not anything to show more fair:
Dull would he be of soul who could pass by
A sight so touching in its majesty.
This city now doth like a garment wear
The beauty of the morning; silent, bare,   5
Ships, towers, domes, theatres, and temples lie
Open to the fields, and to the sky,
All bright and glittering in the smokeless air.
Never did sun more beautifully steep,
In his first splendour, valley, rock, or hill;   10
Ne'er saw I, never felt, a calm so deep!
The river glideth at his own sweet will:
Dear God! the very houses seem asleep;
And all that mighty heart is lying still!

Title, Westminster Bridge: In London, England.

Bernard Barton (1784-1849)

The butterfly, which sports on gaudy wing;
The brawling brooklet, lost in foam and spray,
As it goes dancing in its idle way;
The sunflower, in broad daylight glistening;
Are types of her who in the festive ring   5
Lives but to bask in fashion's vain display,
And glittering through her bright but useless day,
"Flaunts, and goes down a disregarded thing!"
Thy emblem, Lucy, is the busy bee,
Whose industry for future hours provides;   10
The gentle streamlet, gladding as it glides
Unseen along; the flower which gives the lea
Fragrance and loveliness, are types of thee,
And of the active worth thy modest merit hides.

Lines 5, 9, types, emblem: symbols, symbol
Line 8, "Flaunts. . .": A rough quotation from Alexander Pope, *Moral Essays*, II, line 252.

John Keats (1795-1821)

On First Looking Into Chapman's Homer

Much have I travelled in the realms of gold,
And many goodly states and kingdoms seen;
Round many islands have I been,
Which bards in fealty to Apollo hold.
Oft of one wide expanse had I been told   5
That deep-browed Homer ruled as his demesne;
Yet never did I breathe its pure serene
Till I heard Chapman speak out loud and bold:
Then felt I like some watcher of the skies,
When a new planet swims into his ken;   10
Or like stout Cortez when with eagle eyes
He stared at the Pacific–and all his men
Looked at each other with a wild surmise–
Silent, upon a peak in Darien.

Title, Chapman's Homer: George Chapman (c. 1559-1634) published in 1616 the first complete translation into English of Homer's *Iliad* and *Odyssey*.
Lines 11-12, Cortez . . . Pacific: A Spanish conquistador, Hernán Cortés (1485-1547) led an expedition that led to the fall of the Aztec empire. Actually, men of an expedition under Vasco Núñez de Balboa (c. 1475-1519) were the first Europeans to see the Pacific Ocean.
Line 14, Darien: The Darién province of Panama.

Henry Alford (1810-1871)

Rise, said the Master, come unto the feast:
She heard the call, and rose with willing feet;
But thinking it not otherwise than meet
For such a bidding to put on her best,
She is gone from us for a few short hours   5
Into her bridal closet, there to wait
For the unfolding of the palace gate
That gives her entrance to the blissful bowers.
We have not seen her yet, though we have been
Full often to her chamber door, and oft   10
Have listened underneath the postern green,
And laid fresh flowers, and whispered short and soft:
But she made no answer; and the day
From the clear west is fading fast away.

John Clare (1793-1864)

Farewell

Farewell to the bushy clump close to the river
And the flags where the butter-bump hides in forever;
Farewell to the weedy brook, hemmed in by waters;
Farewell to the miller's brook and his three bonny daughters;
Farewell to them all while in prison I lie–　　　　　　　5
In the prison a thrall sees naught but the sky.

Shut out are the green fields and birds in the bushes;
In the prison yard nothing builds, blackbirds or thrushes.
Farewell to the old mill and dash of the waters,
To the miller and, dearer still, to his three bonny daughters.　　10

In the nook, the larger burdock grows near the green willow;
In the flood, round the moor-cock dashes under the billow;
To the old mill farewell, to the lock, pens, and waters,
To the miller himsel', and his three bonny daughters.

Title, Farewell: In 1837 John Clare took up residence in a mental asylum, of his own volition. He passed almost the entire remainder of his life under confinement.
Line 2, butter-bump: bittern.

Walt Whitman (1819-1892)

Patroling Barnegat

Wild, wild the storm, and the sea high running,
Steady the roar of the gale, with incessant undertone muttering,
Shouts of demoniac laughter fitfully piercing and pealing,
Waves, air, midnight, their savagest trinity lashing,
Out in the shadows there milk-white combs careering, 5
On beachy slush and sand spirts of snow fierce slanting,
Where through the murk the easterly death-wind breasting,
Through cutting swirl and spray watchful and firm advancing,
(That in the distance! is that a wreck? is the red signal flaring?)
Slush and sand of the beach tireless till daylight wending, 10
Steadily, slowly, through hoarse roar never remitting,
Along the midnight edge by those milk-white combs careering,
A group of dim, weird forms, struggling, the night confronting,
That savage trinity warily watching.

Title, Barnegat: Barnegat Bay, off the east coast of New Jersey.

Emma Lazarus (1849-1887)

The New Colossus

Not like the brazen giant of Greek fame,
With conquering limbs astride from land to land;
Here at our sea-washed, sunset gates shall stand
    A mighty woman with a torch, whose flame
    Is the imprisoned lightning, and her name   5
    Mother of Exiles. From her beacon-hand
Glows world-wide welcome; her mild eyes command
    The air-bridged harbor that twin cities frame.
"Keep, ancient lands, your storied pomp!" cries she
With silent lips. "Give me your tired, your poor,   10
Your huddled masses yearning to breathe free,
    The wretched refuse of your teeming shore.
Send these, the homeless, tempest-tost to me,
I lift my lamp beside the golden door!"

Title, Colossus: One of the Seven Wonders of the ancient world, the Colossus of Rhodes was erected in the third century B.C. The statue, representing the Greek Titan Helios, was over 100 feet high. Legs spread, it bestrode two columns as it looked out over the sea.

Line 4, a mighty woman with a torch: The Statue of Liberty, in New York Harbor, was dedicated in 1886. Lazarus wrote this sonnet in 1883 to assist in an effort to raise funds for construction of a foundation to support the statue.

Helena Coleman (1860-1953)

Among the Mountains

As far as sight could reach the wild peaks rose,
Tier after tier against the limpid blue,
Titanic forms that stormed the heavens anew
At every turn, crowned with imperial snows;
And then, as day sank softly to its close, 5
Diaphanous, ethereal they grew,
Mere wraiths of rainbow-mist that from our view,
Dream-laden, lapsed to darkness and repose.
And suddenly I found my vision blurred,
And know that deeper chord was touched again 10
Which once in Hungary, when I had heard
A passionately wild, appealing strain
Of gypsy music, left me strangely stirred
With incommunicable joy and pain.

Line 3, Titanic forms: In Greek mythology, the Titans were powerful gods that ruled the earth during the Golden Age. They were overthrown in war with a younger generation of gods, the Olympians.

Sophie Jewett (pseudonym of Ellen Burroughs, 1861-1909)

Thoughts

The morning brought a stranger to my door,
I know not whence such feet as his may stray,
From what still heights, along what star-set way.
A child he seemed, yet my eyes fell before
His eyes Olympian. I did implore   5
Him enter, linger but one golden day
To bless my house. He passed, he might not stay,
And though I call with tears, he comes no more.

At noon there stole a beggar to my gate,
Of subtle tongue, the porter he beguiled.   10
His creeping evil steps my house defiled.
I flung him scornful alms, I bade him straight
To leave me. Swift he clutched my fee and smiled,
Yet went not forth, nor goes, despite my hate.

Line 5, Olympian: Mount Olympus, the highest mountain in Greece, was regarded by the ancients as the home of the gods.

Robinson Jeffers (1887-1962)

Eucalyptus Trees

Thankful, my country, be to him who first
Brought hither from Australia oversea
Sapling or seed of the undeciduous tree
Whose grave and sombre foliage fears no burst
Of heat from summer-naked heavens, nor thirst   5
Though all the winter is rainless, and the bee
Starves, finding not a blossom. Patiently
The great roots delve, and feel though deep-immersed
Some layer of ancient moisture, and the leaves
Perish not, hanging pointed in the sky.   10
To see these lofty trunks gray-barked and broad
Wall with clear shade a long white southern road
I have been as one devoted, who receives
An impulse or a promise from on high.

Chapter 6. Groups of Lines

Varying arrangements of two, three, four, and six lines combine to make up the fourteen lines of a sonnet. In this chapter we discuss these groups of lines in succession, concluding with description of the rhyme schemes in the two prevalent sonnet forms, the Shakespearean and the Petrarchan.

In the two-line pattern, known as the *couplet*, the sounds at the ends of lines are usually exact rhymes. The couplet is a versatile medium for poems of any length. When used by itself it is known as the *heroic couplet*, after the types of writing that prevailed at the time of its rise to popularity in English, in the later seventeenth century. By making use of *run-on lines*, or *enjambment*, wherein the sense of one line flows into the next without interruption, writers such as John Dryden (1631-1700) and Alexander Pope wielded the couplet with such skill that they left their readers only half-aware of the steady echoing of rhyme sounds at the ends of verses. But they also took advantage of the two-line form's capacity for crisp formulation. For example, Dryden's mock-heroic poem, *Mac Flecknoe*, begins this way:

> All human things are subject to decay,
> And when fate summons, monarchs must obey.

In a sonnet, couplets occur either in the final two lines, where they round out the ideas that have been developed, or else as parts of longer units that come earlier.

To begin this chapter's practice in composition, try writing a few pentameter couplets. Make the first line end-stopped in at least one of them, and insert a caesura in at least one.

A system in general use to trace the pattern of end-rhymes in a poem is to assign letters to rhyme sounds in the order of their appearance–a, b, c, and so on. Some sonnets extend the sequence as far as to g.

Several three-line rhyme patterns may occur in sonnets, the simplest of which is the *triplet*. In that form the poet uses the same, or approximately the same sound at the end of each line. An example is in "The Love Song of J. Alfred Prufrock" by T.S. Eliot (1888-1965):

> Shall I part my hair behind? Do I dare to eat a peach?
> I shall wear white flannel trousers, and walk upon the beach.
> I have heard the mermaids singing, each to each.

Although frequently encountered in other forms of verse, triplets are not often found in sonnets. The same is true of another well-known pattern, known as *terza rima*, wherein three-line groupings are interlinked, as follows: a, b, a, b, c, b, c, d, c–and so on. This rhyme scheme, which Dante employed in his *Divine Comedy*, has attracted English writers including Shelley, who used it in *Ode to the West Wind*. Of course, a sonnet's brevity affords limited opportunity to realize the continued effect of intertwined rhymes that characterizes terza rima.

The final six lines, called the *sestet*, of a Petrarchan sonnet include three sets of two-line rhyme units, c d c d c d, or two sets of three-line units, c d e c d e, or else some other combination usually involving three rhymes, c d e. A group of sonnets by the American poet Edna St. Vincent Millay (1892-1950) includes examples of each pattern. First, c d e c d e:

> Like him who day by day unto his draught [pronounced *draft*]
> Of delicate poison adds him one drop more
> Till he may drink unharmed the death of ten,
> Even so, inured to beauty, who have quaffed
> Each hour more deeply than the hour before,
> I drink–and live–what has destroyed some men.

Next, c d c d c d; this poem deals with a beloved person no longer with the speaker:

> You go no more on your exultant feet
> Up paths that only mist and morning knew,
> Or watch the wind, or listen to the beat
> Of a bird's wings too high in air to view,–
> But you were something more than young and sweet
> And fair–and the long year remembers you.

The c d e e c d pattern in the lines that follow includes a couplet, whose chiming sounds emphasize a painfully remembered image:

> There are a hundred places where I fear
> To go,–so with his memory they brim!
> And entering with relief some quiet place
> Where never fell his foot nor shone his face
> I say, "There is no memory of him here!"
> And so stand stricken, so remembering him!

One of the satisfactions of writing in the Petrarchan sonnet form is the freedom its sestet affords to select a rhyme scheme that best fits one's intention.

Your next stint of composition practice is to write pentameter lines in groups of three–a a a (triplet); a b a followed by b c b (terza rima)–or two times three–c d e c d e; a b a b a b–or something else. Take your time, and let your inventive self have free rein.

Sonnets typically begin with a four-line rhyme pattern, known as a *quatrain*, followed by another; when combined, the two sets of lines are called the *octave*. In a *Shakespearean sonnet*, the initial quatrain rhymes a b a b, and the one that follows rhymes c d c d. The final line of the first quatrain may be run-on or end-stopped.

An example of a Shakespearean octave is a comic sonnet by an American writer, Elizabeth Akers Allen (1832-1911), who wrote under the pseudonym Florence Percy:

> Strange Truth and Beauty are enemies,
> Treading forever on each other's toes!
> Strange rhymes are always of that which is
> Too false or silly to be said in prose!
> Now here's a sonnet by our village poet
> "Inscribed to Kate," in most romantic style,
> Whereas–and one with half an eye might know it,–
> He means Sophronia Tomkins, all the while.

In the Shakespearean form the initial quatrains usually present separate subunits of thought; however, a great many exceptions make this generalization rough-edged at best.

In a *Petrarchan sonnet*, the matter introduced in the first four lines ordinarily flows without interruption into the second, so that the octave forms a unit. In many cases, the initial eight lines pose a problem or describe a situation; then the concluding six offer a resolution, present another point of view, or otherwise stand apart from what began the sonnet. The usual rhyme scheme of a Petrarchan octave is a b b a a b b a. Whereas the Shakespearean form introduces four rhyme sounds in its octave, the Petrarchan relies on only two, presenting its author a somewhat greater challenge.

Henry Wadsworth Longfellow (1807-1882) was a master at making rhymed verses seem utterly natural. His "Sonnet: Chimes" includes a graceful example of the Petrarchan octave:

> Sweet chimes! that in the loneliness of night
> Salute the passing hour, and in the dark
> And silent chambers of the household mark
> The movements of the myriad orbs of light!
> Through my closed eyelids, by the inner sight,
> I see the constellations in the arc
> Of their great circles moving on, and hark!
> I almost hear them singing in their flight.

The practice session that follows concludes our survey of the structural elements of sonnet writing–words and phrases, lines and rhymes, and groups of lines. We have examined the pieces, large and small, that combine to form a completed sonnet. We are almost ready to assemble the puzzle, and then perhaps to assemble it many times again as new thoughts and the Muse may inspire us.

Try your hand at these four suggested tasks. Again, take your time.

1. Write a pentameter quatrain that incorporates a rhyme scheme of a b a b.

2. Write a pentameter quatrain whose subject connects with what you wrote for the preceding task, but incorporating two different rhymes, c d c d. If you run into trouble, consider going back to the earlier quatrain and starting over.

3. Write a pentameter quatrain that incorporates a rhyme scheme of a b b a.

4. Write a pentameter quatrain whose subject connects with what you wrote for the preceding task, but now incorporating a second iteration of the a b b a pattern. If you run into trouble, consider going back to the earlier quatrain and starting over. Or ask yourself, would these two sets of four lines work better if I reversed all or part of their order?

The traditional format for a Shakespearean sonnet is three pentameter quatrains, rhyming a b a b, then c d c d, and then e f e f, concluding with a couplet, g g. Here is a sample, by a contemporary of Shakespeare, Michael Drayton (1563-1631):

Since there's no help, come let us kiss and part,	a
Nay, I have done, ye get no more of me,	b
And I am glad, yea glad with all my heart	a
That thus so cleanly I myself can free;	b
Shake hands forever, cancel all our vows,	c
And when we meet at any time again,	d
Be it not seen in either of our brows	c
That we one jot of former love retain.	d
Now at the last gasp of love's latest breath,	e
When, his pulse failing, passion speechless lies,	f
When faith is kneeling by his bed of death,	e
And innocence is closing up his eyes,	f
Now if thou would'st, when all have given him over,	g
From death to life thou mightst him yet recover.	g

The traditional format for a Petrarchan sonnet is a pentameter octave, rhyming a b b a a b b a, followed by a sestet, rhyming c d e c d e, c d c d c d, or in some other combination. Here is another example by Henry W. Longfellow. It is entitled "Mezzo Cammin" (midway in the road of life), after a phrase from the first line of Dante's *Divine Comedy,* a poem Longfellow later translated into English. At the time he wrote this sonnet, he was thirty-five years of age and about to return home from Europe. The loss of his wife a few years before had desolated him.

Half of my life is gone, and I have let	a
The years slip by me and have not fulfilled	b
The aspiration of my youth, to build	b
Some tower of song with lofty parapet.	a
Not indolence, nor the pleasure, nor the fret	a
Of restless passions that would not be stilled,	b
But sorrow, and care that almost killed,	b
Kept me from what I may accomplish yet;	a
Though, half way up the hill, I see the Past	c
Lying beneath me with its sounds and sights,	d
A city in the twilight dim and vast,	c
With smoking roofs, soft bells, and gleaming lights,	d
And hear above me on the autumnal blast	c
The cataract of Death far thundering from the heights.	d

The next chapter will offer suggestions as you fashion a sonnet in each of these two forms–first the Shakespearean, then the Petrarchan.

Chapter 7. Drafting and Revising

Sometimes the creative spirit flows through us of its own will, seemingly without effort on our part. I recall occasions when, at the end of a productive day of writing, I knew I had been granted temporary access to a mysterious gift. More often, composition is labor–sentence by sentence, line by scratched out line. And there are times when our wells of inspiration simply go dry.

Complaints about "writer's block" need to be taken seriously, for they signal a prolonged state of creative paralysis that can be deeply distressing. Fortunately, in most cases the condition can be remedied. The elixir that dispels it is a mixture of modest self-confidence and determination to push ahead. What we write during a dry time may not be destined for admiration through the ages, but it will at least produce something to work with later–if not to revise, then to look over and rethink. "Just do it," the upbeat motto broadcast by a maker of athletic equipment, is a good mantra for a frustrated sonnet writer. Another is the phrase everyone remembers from *The Little Engine That Could*, "I think I can."

Writing sonnets was a popular pastime in the later nineteenth and earlier twentieth centuries. Inevitably, lists of rules were formulated at that time to ensure that writers observed guidelines that defined the "perfect" sonnet. One of the codes included seventeen numbered items; another, twenty-one. Nowadays we should distance ourselves from elaborate standards of practice like these, except as historical curiosities, for they shackle the creative impulse.

True, part of a sonnet's beauty is its deft resolution of various problems associated with its traditional form. A successful sonnet develops a single course of thought to a length that fits neatly within its fourteen lines. Its expressions are neither stretched out to fill unneeded space nor tortured into a tight verbal corset. Its sounds and its sense complement each other. It observes one of two traditional rhyme schemes, or some variation thereof. Beyond these general guidelines, our criteria ought to be questions like these: How does it sound? Does it hang together? What could be improved? Rules are to be respected but not revered in sonnet writing.

So, what should I write about? A subject may present itself to you at once: security at the airport; applying makeup; making the team; fog; a lost animal; a remembered look on someone's face. If it doesn't, relax and let your mind survey its scene in wide focus. If necessary, sleep on the matter. You'll come up with something.

While drafting this chapter, I recorded my own experiences as I composed a Shakespearean sonnet. The idea was to make use of those observations as I discussed the stages in your process of drafting. So here, in italics and for what value you may find in it, is where my thought process began. *I happened to recall an unused packet of printed invitations, produced probably in the 1960s, to a cocktail party. The front cover of each card showed a slightly tilted martini glass, complete with toothpick and green olive, and the words "Please join us for cocktails." Inside, printed lines enabled the sender to write in the time and place of the coming event. For me this little artifact conjured up memory of a whole suburban culture, and I took the idea from there. My sonnet could provide only a glimpse at that social scene, but it seemed worth the writing.*

Should you give your sonnet a title, and perhaps a subtitle? Practices differ. During the nineteenth century, writers often supplied titles. If their poems dealt with explicitly personal matters, they also recorded the dates and places of the experiences they described. In my opinion, assigning a title ought to come at the very end of one's effort, if it comes at all. After all, one cannot know what a sonnet will say until he or she finishes it. Ordinarily, by the way, a sonnet without title is referred to by its first line or, if it forms part of a sequence, its number in that series. *When I had finished my lines about the cocktail party, the phrase "Society Verse" occurred to me, and I liked it well enough to keep it.*

What writing instruments and medium should you use while drafting your sonnet? Some persons like to compose at a computer screen, for example. I cannot imagine successful composition being done that way, but there you are. Especially when I am at work on prose writings, my computer does seems to me a wonderful tool for revising and editing, a great advantage over revising on paper, retyping, then revising again *ad infinitum*. But for the first draft or two, I find that writing by hand is the only true method. This is even more the case when I write verse. I prefer a long sheet of paper, say 8 ½ x 14 inches, with wide spacing between the ruled lines. I write out my text with double spacing, leaving plenty of room for revisions between the lines, and I try not to fill up the sheet so that it's messy and I lose track of things. I use the blank spaces for stray thoughts, possible rhymes, alternative word choices–whatever occurs that might come in handy. I like pencil, not ink. Ordinarily I cross out a false start rather than erasing it, because if it's still visible I can go back and reconsider it.

I don't make a fair copy–that is, a fresh copy, of the lines that are evolving, until the first page is pretty well filled. When I set aside that first page, I save it until the sonnet is on the cusp of final form, and then I throw it away. Trashing my art, as it were, can be difficult, because the working pages sometimes trace a process that is interesting in retrospect. However, it's a practice I've become comfortable with, because probably I'm the only person interested in recalling how the poem came into being. Besides, my house doesn't need more litter.

Where and when should you do your writing? You know best about the circumstances that make you comfortable. It's good to have a dictionary close at hand, and to find a place that promises few distractions. Some of us are at our best in the morning, others late at night. Not long ago a novelist remarked that during a day his compositional high point occurred shortly after the midday meal, when the wine he had drunk left him still elevated but not yet sleepy. Whenever you write, it's good to remember that you can return to a work-in-progress whenever you please. After all, it's possible to work for too long at a sitting. By taking a break, you let your mind refresh itself.

Understand that once you begin writing, your mind will be operating in parallel, on two levels at once; call them the conscious and the subconscious. One will busy itself with counting syllables, selecting and arranging words, trimming and tailoring. The other will do its work out of sight, rummaging, unearthing, recalling, and sorting. The two will interact, but you need to let them both operate in their own way. That's why it's a good idea to jot down ideas when they do float into your consciousness, and before you even comprehend why they did.

Will you begin your sonnet with an apostrophe? Do you have certain phrases all ready to go, just waiting for their placement? What will be your prevailing tone? Do you intend to spin out an allegory? These are all good questions, but it's best not to answer them firmly before you start writing. Most often, sonnet writers find that they end up saying something rather different from what they thought they would at first. One of the pleasures of reading through a well-turned Shakespearean sonnet is observing how it moves toward its final couplet, knowing that those final lines will neatly sum things up. But the situation is quite different for a writer; he or she cannot know how the sonnet-in-progress will end until those last lines are at hand, and even then they need to be formulated and fine-tuned. Experienced sonnet writers understand the need to second-guess themselves at every point, considering all their options.

Drafting the first line or two can be the most agonizing stage of writing a sonnet. To avoid the onset of writer's block, push yourself to get started. You have decided on a general subject, so now set down something connected with it that prospectively interests or amuses you. Write down some words, rhymes, images, names that might serve, then look it all over and write some more. You are already thinking of what might follow. Write a line or two, a bit long or short if that's how they present themselves, and see what you have.

I began with three start-offs: "Come over for cocktails!"; "We've been invited for cocktails"; and "Please join us for cocktails!" All seemed practicable, placing us in the middle of a social situation. I tried out the first one, then decided on the third, continuing thus:

> "Please join us for cocktails!" Well, why not?
> They aren't a bad couple.

Not *is an easy word to rhyme with, I told myself with satisfaction, and then, more or less simultaneously, I had the idea of looking over a list of possible attendees in order to* **spot** *any unwelcome names. Hurrah! a rhyme. The next few lines came easily:*

> We'll discreetly
> Check out who else is going, and if we spot
> Any Black Flags on the list, we can neatly
> Send our regrets.

This was progress. A little story is getting told. The feminine rhymes have set a light tone.

Now, your turn. If you can write out a quatrain, a b a b, that satisfies you at least for now, great. If not, let the project simmer and keep at it until you've come that far. Beginning a sonnet is like diving into a swimming pool of suspicious water temperature. Take the plunge, and you'll soon be comfortable.

Now, quatrain number two, which will develop what we've begun and may lead to a turning point at the end of the octave. In your poem you perhaps started a list that you can continue–of ideas, beliefs, persons, relations, events, whatever. You may have presented one side of an argument, possibly his beef with her, and now you can turn to hers with him. However you began, we're afloat, so we paddle ahead. We do need a couple of new rhymes.

I had no serious trouble with my second quatrain until I had drafted the whole sonnet and realized that I had failed to count my lines correctly. You'll recall that my Send our regrets begins line 5; I must have thought it was line 4, because beginning with the fifth line I ended lines as follows: hope, song, know, strong, snow, go. I knew my first lines had gone past the quatrain break, which I had intended to observe with an end-stopped line, but somehow I got confused. I went back and re-wrote the last half of line 5 through line 8:

> *Mustn't burn bridges, right?*
> *Ask around, so we can have a roster to review.*
> *I don't expect heavy hitters or bright*
> *Lights, but you might turn up a new name or two.*

Once I had made the repairs, which required that I sleep on the problem and fix it next morning, these lines seemed to me satisfactory. The tone is still casual, cautious, a little dismissive of the whole social situation. But the plot thickens; we await the list of attendees. I decided to insert a space between my second and third quatrains, to signify Before and After.

Your turn now for the second quatrain. Of course, whether you choose to finish it with an end-stopped line or not is up to you. If you want to continue your a b a b rhyme scheme instead of going on to c d c d, go ahead, if you think there's something to be gained. Don't trouble yourself about those graybeards with their lists of seventeen ways to make mistakes.

I sometimes use a programmable exercise machine that beeps me an upbeat message once I have completed the timed workout I have punched in. "Good job!" the visual display assures me, in fluorescent script. I spare you that insincere applause, but I am happy to point out that, having now written eight lines, you are more than halfway to your goal. Already you are thinking of how you'll end the sonnet. Indeed, this is a question that should start shadowing your mind at this point.

Quatrain three is too late in the game to insert something entirely new, unless of course that forms part of your plan. The sudden thought of an old lover breaks a mood; an accident occurs; something hurtful is said–any of these could force a change of direction in exactly the way you wish. But lines usually 9 through 14 present either a continuation or a reversal, which is a kind of continuation. The lines clearly relate to what came before them, and the tone of your poem does not modulate much.

After drafting my third quatrain, I wrote this note about my thought process while at work on it: "Still wasn't sure whether they'd accept the invitation. They will, I've decided that, but I don't know my angle for the ending." With a few adjustments, my lines 9 through 12 came out as you might expect. I kept up the implied team metaphor, returned to the hyperbole of Black Flags in line 4, maintained the tone of slightly superior irony:

> *So, a respectable list, lengthwise at least,*
> *Pretty much the same suburban squad*
> *We've come to consort with. No barbarous beasts,*
> *No divas, nobody thought really odd.*

Here is space for your draft of the third quatrain:

Well, by now your sonnet has taken a very different course from mine, and let us both rejoice in the difference. We stand together, ready to formulate a conclusion that will ring like silver. What shall we write? Concluding with a question is a perfectly respectable course, if an open-ended effect is what you want. Hugh R. Evans' "The Veld" (page 40) ends in that way, very effectively. The final couplet should connect on some way with has led up to it, and should confer a feeling of completion if not resolution.

I had serious difficulty completing my sonnet, even though I had decided that the invitation to the cocktail party was to be accepted. First I thought of placing the couplet within quotation marks, perhaps as the couple's response to the invitation. Then I thought of briefly portraying their debate together about whether to accept or decline. I thought of general reflections they might indulge in, once they had decided to attend. And all along, I wrote down possible phrases, with rhymes to enclose them. It was all rather frustrating. Taking out a fresh sheet of paper, I wrote "Thought, no fruit yet." I tried this couplet: "It's good to stay in touch with the folks you know, / And a cocktail party's the perfect place to go," then asked myself, "Which line first?"

At some point I decided to quit searching for a generalization about the question whether to accept the invitation. Instead I would look for a firm, go-for-it statement of willingness to attend. Here are two of my feeble efforts in that direction:

No matter what they're serving, whisky, gin,
Or something more modish, we should fit right in.

Whatever they're serving—whisky, gin,
Rum, wine coolers—we should fit right in.

I did like "fit right in," and after a few moment I recalled a phrase that connected with the sports metaphor above: "Let the games begin." I had a set of rhymes!

But I was still tinkering with that couplet as I sat down to type out the sonnet. Just then I recalled an expression my parents liked to use, "We'll be there with bells on," signifying their delight at the anticipation of a good time somewhere. That mental bolt from the blue ended my search. Wearing bells has always suggested to me the costume of a court fool, with his cap and bells, and it think it does for other people as well. Using the phrase would enable me to turn the spotlight of wry irony on my speaker, who had been directing it toward others in his neighborhood. My poem ended this way:

Bring on the cocktails, I say, let the party begin.
We'll be there with bells on, and we'll fit right in.

I hope your attempt to hit upon a concluding couplet will tax your patience less than mine did. But, having come this far, it's time to finish up.

So, congratulations! Have you decided whether to include a title? The space below is for you to consider a few possibilities. When you've made your choice, use the blank page that follows to write down a fair copy of your Shakespearean sonnet. I'll print mine on the page that follows. Probably like you, I have no illusion that my poem will qualify me to consideration for any grand prize, but I am glad I made the effort to write it. The expenditure of mental energy was, for me, well worth the making.

Your Shakespearean sonnet:

Society Verse

"Please join us for cocktails." Well, why not?
They aren't a bad couple. We'll discreetly
Check out who else is going, and if we spot
Any Black Flags on the list, we can neatly
Send our regrets. Mustn't burn bridges, right?
Ask around, so we can have a roster to review.
I don't expect heavy hitters or bright
Lights, but you might turn up a new name or two.

So, a respectable list, lengthwise at least,
Pretty much the same suburban squad
We've come to consort with. No barbarous beasts,
No divas, nobody thought really odd.
Bring on the cocktails, I say, let the party begin.
We'll be there with bells on, and we'll fit right in.

By now we surely agree that writing a sonnet is not a merely mechanical process. Far from it! Let me recommend to you "The Philosophy of Composition" by Edgar Allan Poe (1809-1849), an essay which purports, brilliantly, to demonstrate that "accident or intuition" played no part whatever in his writing of "The Raven," a poem 108 lines long, and with an elaborate rhyme scheme. Rather, he claims, "the work proceeded step by step to its completion with the precision and rigid consequence of a mathematical problem." Poe's essay is a fine performance, and contains much truth; and yet we cannot take it seriously as a comprehensive statement about the creative process, any more than we can believe that a poet writes his or her lines while in the throes of some fine frenzy. The truth lies somewhere between the two extremes.

Next, we compose a Petrarchan sonnet. The octave, with lines rhyming a b b a a b b a, has a fixed pattern that includes three couplets. The sestet's rhyme scheme is yours to decide. This freedom to arrange the latter lines according to one's will may account in part for the popularity of Petrarchan sonnets. They are less well known to the general reading audience than the Shakespearean form, but more of them get published.

The problems one faces in choosing a subject, writing the initial lines, and moving forward within the structure are essentially the same for the two forms, so we will abbreviate the approach we took with the Shakespearean sonnet. However, I do have a few experiences to relate about the Petrarchan sonnet I wrote for this chapter, and I hope some of them may prove useful to you.

Once I had decided to write something about getting fit, and visiting an up-to-date health spa, I brainstormed for rhymes. I liked feminine endings for the light touch they could lend. Some samples of what I wrote in my initial notes are robotizer, analyzer, digitizer, breathalyzer, wiser; ready, steady, bready, pedi, sleddy, already; run yet, sun set, fun yet, done yet, won yet. Another rhyme list included oohs and ahs, Dr. Oz, laws, claws, blahs. I had plenty to work with, rhymewise, and drafting the octave proved easy going. Here's what I produced:

> *Restless in a rut of late stage blahs,*
> *My girlish gait grown awkward and unsteady,*
> *My torso, limbs, and whatnot frankly bready,*
> *I decided to live by the lightfoot laws*
> *Of healthy living taught by Doctor Oz*
> *And the buff instructors at our spa. Already*
> *I felt better. No more ice cream and spaghetti,*
> *But some perky glutes, flat abs, lots of oohs and ahs.*

It's time now to write your draft of the Petrarchan octave.

The rhyme scheme you choose for the sestet will likely differ from mine, but I'm sure my experience in setting it up will resemble yours to some degree.

I decided on c d c d c d as my pattern, drew upon my list of rhymes, and drafted my six lines. I was reasonably satisfied with all but the last two, which kept tickling my mind:

>*Readout in hand from the robot analyzer,*
>*I first slowed down the treadmill, not ready to run yet.*
>*Then, warmed up, I turned on the jazzerciser*
>*And bounded around, it seemed until sunset.*
>*I was exhausted but not yet fitter or wiser.*
>*I asked myself, "Am I having fun yet?"*

The word wiser *bothered me because it didn't really fit; I was writing about fitness, not wisdom. The concluding question seemed a little trite but not really objectionable.*

After adjusting a few details, I printed out the sonnet and set it aside, still not fully satisfied. I had thought of lither *(more lithe) instead of* wiser, *but it seemed too odd, especially after* bready *in line 3. Days passed, and then* thinner *occurred to me, and* winner. *Here was an opportunity, even though working the words into a final couplet would mean discarding my c d c d c d plan. I tried various combinations, and finally some ideas surfaced that enabled me to complete the poem in a way I liked. That breakthrough resulted in a review of the whole sonnet, which in turn led to improvements and a final draft. I had entitled the earlier draft "Life Change" and decided to keep it.*

Life Change

Restless in a rut of late stage blahs,
My torso, limbs, and whatnot frankly bready,
My girlish gait grown awkward and unsteady,
I decided to live by the lightfoot laws
Of healthy living taught by Doctor Oz   5
And the buff instructors at our spa. Already
I felt better. No more ice cream and spaghetti,
But some perky glutes, flat abs, lots of oohs and ahs.

So, readout in hand from the robot analyzer,
I walked on the treadmill, not ready to run yet.   10
Then, warmed up, I turned on the jazzerciser
And bounded around–it seemed until sunset.
At last, a machine voice: "Done! You're a winner!"
Workout complete, I turned my attention to dinner.

As you notice, I sacrificed my final c d for a couplet, as in a Shakespearean sonnet. I think the couplet produces a better ending and a better sonnet, by a little, than I had before. Will lightning strike, in retribution for my rhyme scheme heterodoxy? I doubt it.

Now, see where your first intentions for your Petrarchan sestet take you. As you proceed, you might enjoy tracing your thought process in writing the last six lines.

Like the delicate mechanism of a wristwatch, a sonnet runs properly only when adjusted with care. It's difficult to say just when revision of a poem should end. Once you begin serious work on the lines, they will echo inside your head, especially if you aren't yet happy with them. They won't stop bothering you, so you may as well take another look at your latest version and see what can be done. The time to stop revising is when you're no longer able to tell whether your changes are resulting in improvements.

Should you solicit the advice of others as you write successive drafts? No answer will suit every case, except "Maybe." On one hand, as an author you struggle to maintain objectivity while fondly admiring your brainchild. And for this very reason, any phrase, image, turn of thought, coinage, or rhyme that you especially like should be suspect. You should examine it with a wary eye, and you might also benefit from dispassionate appraisal by another person whose judgment you trust. After all, a completed poem assumes a reader. If you intend to make your work available to an audience, you want it to convey its message in the best way possible.

On the other hand, showing a work-in-progress to someone else is a delicate personal and interpersonal matter. Another individual's response to your writing may give you no assistance at all. In fact, it may muddy the water, leave you in creative limbo, and even sour a friendship. I keep to myself the things I write until I'm virtually finished with them–unless, as in this book, the plan is to share my experiences with someone who is involved in the same process.

Write out the fair copy of your Petrarchan sonnet on the blank page that follows.

Your Petrarchan sonnet:

Chapter 8. One Last Dozen Sonnets

The poems in this chapter can best be appreciated by readers, and especially writers, of sonnets. All portray either the power of sonnets or else the process of writing them. Some will impress, others will amuse, and all should resonate with you in light of your experience as a sonnet writer.

William Shakespeare (1554-1616), Sonnet 55

Not marble, nor the gilded monuments
Of princes, shall outlive this powerful rhyme;
But you shall shine more bright in these conténts
Than unswept stone, besmeared with sluttish time.
When wasteful war shall statues overturn,
And broils root out the work of masonry,
Nor Mars his sword nor war's quick fire shall burn
The living record of your memory.
'Gainst death and all-oblivious enmity
Shall you pace forth; your praise shall still find room
Even in the eyes of all posterity
That wear this world out to the ending doom.
So, till the judgment that yourself arise,
You live in this, and dwell in lovers' eyes.

Line 13, the judgment that yourself arise: the Last Judgment.

William Shakespeare, Sonnet 107

Not mine own fears, nor the prophetic soul
Of the wide world dreaming on things to come,
Can yet the lease of my true love control,
Supposed as forfeit to a cónfined doom.
The mortal moon hath her eclipse endured,
And the sad augurs mock their own presage;
Incertainties now crown themselves assured,
And peace proclaims olives of endless age.
Now with the drops of this most balmy time
My love looks fresh, and death to me subscribes,
Since, spite of him, I'll live in this poor rhyme,
While he insults o'er dull and speechless tribes:
And thou in this shalt find thy monument,
When tyrants' crests and tombs of brass are spent.

Lines 1-4: Nothing that foretells an end to my love can be valid.

Edward Williams (1748-1826)

In the Welsh Manner

Dear Nan, at thy command I string a sonnet,
And must in rhyme surpass the Italian skill,
Full fourteen lines with flimsy jingle fill.
What fools we lovers are–I've thus begun it–
The task is hard, but yet I dare not shun it–
I'll persevere and bid the muse distil
Strength in my thought from her inspiring rill,
Till to the length required I've neatly spun it.
But when at length thy fettered bard has done it,
Poor is the thought–the sentiment how chill!
See where he stands! Knight of the dashing quill!
Bewigged a critic, and he'll poop upon it.
But let the witless growler have his will,
I bargained for thy kiss, and have now fairly won it.

Robert Burns (1759-1796)

A Sonnet upon Sonnets

Fourteen, a sonneteer thy praises sings;
What magic myst'ries in that number lie!
Your hen hath fourteen eggs beneath her wings
That fourteen chickens to the roost may fly.
Fourteen full pounds the jockey's stone must be;
His age fourteen–a horse's prime is past.
Fourteen long hours too oft the Bard must fast;
Fourteen bright bumpers–bliss he ne'er must see!
Before fourteen, a dozen yields the strife;
Before fourteen–e'en thirteen's strength is vain.
Fourteen good years–a woman gives us life;
Fourteen good men–we lose that life again.
What lucubrations can be more upon it?
Fourteen good measur'd verses make a sonnet.

Line 5, stone: In Britain, a stone is a unit of weight, fourteen pounds avoirdupois.

William Wordsworth (1770-1850)

Nuns fret not at their convent's narrow room;
And hermits are contented with their cells;
And students with their pensive citadels;
Maids at the wheel, the weaver at his loom,
Sit blithe and happy; bees that soar for bloom,
High as the highest peak of Furness-fells,
Will murmur by the hour in foxglove bells:
In truth the prison, into which we doom
Ourselves, no prison is: and hence for me,
In sundry moods, 'twas pastime to be bound
Within the Sonnet's scanty plot of ground,
Pleased if some Souls (for such there needs must be)
Who have felt the weight of too much liberty,
Should find brief solace there, as I have found.

Line 6, Furness-fells: Mountains in the Lake District of England.

William Wordsworth

Scorn not the sonnet; critic, you have frowned,
Mindless of its just honors; with this key
Shakespeare unlocked his heart; the melody
Of this small lute gave ease to Petrarch's wound;
A thousand times this pipe did Tasso sound;
With it Camöens soothed an exile's grief;
The sonnet glittered a gay myrtle leaf
Amid the cypress with which Dante crowned
His visionary brow; a glow-worm lamp,
It cheered mild Spenser, called from Faeryland
To struggle through dark days; and, when a damp
Fell round the path of Milton, in his hand
The thing became a trumpet; whence he blew
Soul-animating strains–alas, too few!

Lines 4-12, Petrarch's . . . Milton: Francesco Petrarch (1304-1374), Italian author of sonnets in praise of an unattainable woman, Laura; Torquato Tasso (1544-1595), prolific Italian author whose works include more than five hundred love poems; Luis de Camoëns (1524-1580), reputed to be Portugal's greatest poet; Dante Alighieri (c. 1265-1321), among the earliest sonnet writers; Edmund Spenser (1552-1599), author of a sonnet sequence, *Amoretti* (1595); John Milton (1608-1674), author of sonnets high in quality but few in number.

John Dovaston (1782-1854)

The Sonnet

There are who say the sonnet's meted maze
Is all too fettered for the poet's powers,
Compelled to crowd his flush and airy flowers
Like pots of tall imperials, ill at ease.
Or should some tiny thought his fancy seize,
A violet on a vase's top it towers,
And mid the mass of leaves he round it showers
Its little cap and tippet scarce can raise.

Others assert the sonnet's proper praise
Like petalled flowers to each its due degree;
The king-cup five, the pilewort eight bright rays,
The speedwell four, the green-tipped snowdrop three:
So mid the bard's all-petalled sorts is seen
The sonnet–simple flowret of fourteen.

John Keats (1795-1821)

On the Sonnet

If by dull rhymes our English must be chained,
    And, like Andromeda, the Sonnet sweet
Fettered, in spite of painéd loveliness:
Let us find out, if we must be constrained,
    Sandals more interwoven and complete
To fit the naked foot of poesy;
Let us inspect the lyre, and weigh the stress
Of every chord, and see what may be gained
    By ear industrious, and attention meet;
Misers of sound and syllable, no less
Than Midas of his coinage, let us be
    Jealous of dead leaves in the bay-leaf crown;
So, if we may not let the Muse be free,
    She will be bound with garlands of our own.

Line 2, Andromeda: A princess chained to a rock as offering to a sea-monster; Perseus rescued her.
Line 10, Midas: When granted his wish that all he touched should be turned into gold, the mythical king Midas soon repented it.

Dante Gabriel Rossetti (1828-1882)

A Sonnet

A Sonnet is a moment's monument–
    Memorial from the soul's eternity
    To one dead deathless hour. Look that it be,
Whether for lustral rite or dire portent,
Of its own arduous fullness reverent:
    Carve it in ivory or in ebony,
    As Day or Night may rule; and let Time see
Its flowering crest impearled and orient.

A Sonnet is a coin: its face reveals
    The Soul–its converse, to what Power 'tis due:
Whether for tribute to the august appeals
    Of Life, or dower in Love's high retinue,
It serve; or, 'mid the dark wharf's cavernous breath,
In Charon's palm it pay the toll to Death.

Line 14, Charon's palm: After receiving payment, Charon ferried the shades of the newly dead across the river Styx to Hades.

Richard Watson Gilder (1844-1909)

The Sonnet

What is a sonnet? 'Tis the pearly shell
That murmurs of the far-off murmuring sea;
A precious jewel carved most curiously:
It is a little picture painted well.
What is a sonnet? 'Tis the tear that fell
From a great poet's hidden ecstasy;
A two-edged sword, a star, a song–ah me!
Sometimes a heavy-tolling funeral bell.
This was the flame that shook with Dante's breath;
The solemn organ whereon Milton played,
And the clear glass where Shakespeare's shadow falls:
A sea this is–beware who ventureth!
For like a fjord the narrow floor is laid
Mid-ocean deep to the sheer mountain walls.

Edwin Arlington Robinson (1869-1935)

Sonnet

The master and the slave go hand in hand,
Though touch be lost. The poet is a slave,
And there be kings do sorrowfully crave
The joyance that a scullion may command.
But, ah, the sonnet-slave must understand
The mission of his bondage, or the grave
May clasp his bones, or ever he shall save
The perfect word that is the poet's wand.

The sonnet is a crown, whereof the rhymes
Are for Thought's purest gold the jewel-stones;
But shapes and echoes that are never done
Will haunt the workshop, as regret sometimes
Will bring with human yearning to sad thrones
The crash of battles that are never won.

Anonymous

Then and Now

Mourn not the sonnet, for though not now in fashion,
And scorned by writers averse to making rhyme,
Centuries of use have earned it honored station
That ensures its fame will live beyond our time.
Having served well the likes of Spenser, Sidney,
Milton, Wordsworth, Shelley, Hardy, and Frost,
And Shakespeare too–all writers of high kidney,
It's in no danger of dying out or getting lost.

Ah, if I could see my name among those idols,
The author of writings admired some future day!
Thus far, it's true, my practice recitals
Seem awkward apprentice work, try as I may.
Still, the more sonnets I write, the better they get.
An immortal I'm not, I admit, at least not yet.

Chapter 9. Coda

> Gritting my teeth, I set to work upon it,
> And the result's right here, a pretty good sonnet.

On rare occasions a *coda*, or tailpiece, completes a sonnet, bringing its length to sixteen or seventeen lines. The coda comments on the subject matter of the first fourteen lines, often with a comic twist. The couplet above might accurately refer to your participation in this book–except that by now you have written two sonnets, not one.

If the preceding chapters have afforded you pleasure and some good mental exercise, please spread the word–not so much about the merits of this modest volume, but about the rewards sonnet writing has brought you. As you have discovered, the only real investment necessary for a sonnet writer is of time and attention, and the returns can be gratifying. You can pursue your interest when you please, in private or in company with like-minded persons, and the fruits of your effort may prove a source of satisfaction for a long time to come.

This brief introduction may have piqued your interest in forms of short verse other than the sonnet. If so, reading through poetry collections or glancing at published surveys of lyric poetry will guide you to many attractive possibilities–more, in fact, than you can test in a lifetime. Your work with sonnet writing has been a good place to start, and you may well choose to confine your efforts to that form, for a time at least. If you do, note that long series of sonnets can grow tiresome, especially when they churn through roughly the same subject matter, in the same style, in poem after poem. Shorter groupings draw the reader's attention to small differences between their successive units and can be very effective. Most persons agree that the best remembered sonnets were written to stand alone, each being as Dante Gabriel Rossetti expressed it, "a moment's monument."

Make sure you retain copies of the sonnets you write, whether you publish them or not. You may also want to date them and note the circumstances that led you to write them. Stay attuned to events, scenes–any features of the passing hour that capture your interest. Be ready to say to yourself, "I think I'll write a sonnet on it," and then get started.

Printed in Great Britain
by Amazon.co.uk, Ltd.,
Marston Gate.